Old becomes New

Housing Transformation

Dorian Lucas

Old becomes New

Housing Transformation

BRAUN

above: Croft Lodge Studio, p. 170
below: Sand Dune Sanctuary, p. 188

above: Casa Castramao, p. 8
below: Residence at Lerchenberg, p. 88

Although completely new construction has always been the dream of every builder, this was usually not realized for financial reasons over centuries. It was only with classical modernism and the more or less streamlined construction processes of the early 20th century that new construction became the often less expensive solution. This became even more popular in the post-war period. However, with Post-modernism and the squatters of the 1960s and 70s, as well as the European Architectural Heritage Year in 1975, the value of the historical stock was recognized. Then, in the 1980s, historic stucco ceilings became the selling point par excellence and old building fabric was increasingly valued, restored and obviously incorporated into new designs. Today it is common to consider renovation as an alternative to new construction.

Blanket of Steel, p. 130

Koser I, p. 206

Walls can be updated with new insulation, and broken windows can be replaced with triple-pane windows for higher thermal efficiency. There are infinite ways of reusing original resources and infrastructure. At a time of rapid climate change this sustainable approach to building not only reduces waste but also the embodied energy of a house, invested in the manufacturing and delivery of construction materials, as well as the construction process itself. On the issue of soil sealing, making use of the existing plot allows valuable ground and land surfaces to remain permeable and fertile.

Preservation of a building is also a creative challenge that has many different solutions ranging from total restoration to building something almost completely new. The act of balancing conservation with modern elements is highly delicate and subjective to each architect. Approaches to this challenge are also susceptible to the available, existing materials. Structurally unstable ruins are more unsuited for renovation than an esthetically outdated townhouse, but could deliver base materials for new masonry. Functionally upcycling materials to build something new offers the advantage of wide discretion over the end result, as there are no limiting factors such as existing floor plans or strictly designated purposes of materials. In contrast, limitations can also facilitate innovative and clever solutions that might not otherwise have been devised. For example, a part of wall that seems unmotivated can give rise to a new layout or even use of space, and gawky placed windows can lead to new ideas for interior lighting. This sentiment holds especially true for listed buildings that require a careful and extremely conservationist approach. The field of conservation has many different techniques itself. Restoring the building to its original state grants observers a historically accurate experience, transforming a building into a time machine. However, showcasing the historic fabric of a house along with all its flaws within a modern context is sometimes preferred because this is how memories, change of culture, and the passing of time can be showcased. All of these approaches are valid. In fact, their very diversity is the driving force behind housing transformation and its incredible results.

Box House, p. 228

Urban Beat, p. 240

Beyond that are requirements that stem from the very nature of housing: to provide a shelter in hospitable or even inhospitable environments. Since its inception, the purpose of housing has transformed into something more meaningful, something that represents a space of comfort and safety, resting and regeneration: a home. Homes are just as unique as their inhabitants. Over time they both demand different needs to be met, and not all of them are satisfied with preexisting infrastructure. For housing transformations that can mean supplementing the original structures with new annexes or balconies, windows or roofs. The manner in which additions themselves are executed is dependent on the brief of the client and of the architects' vision and imagination.

Accordingly, the rescue, renovation, restoration, and redesign of old buildings is a prestigious task, a sign of our times and a creative act of both designers and clients. This book shows numerous ways to deal with what has been handed down over generations. It presents more than 40 individual and very differently weighted approaches to synchronize the needs of past and present, to update the aesthetic value of what has been left behind, to give a home to new users, to guarantee a future for old stones.

Casa Castromao

Ourense, Spain

After careful rehabilitation, the iconic original layout and consequent shape of the building are legible again.

1

Located in the rural settlement of Castromao, three continuous buildings belonging to Ourense province were abandoned and strongly deteriorated. Their rehabilitation aimed to transform the old farmers' houses into one dwelling by annexing the three spaces that were originally independent while maintaining as much of the original essence of the buildings as possible.

The first step of the rehabilitation process was to identify singular elements of the building in need of restoration. Careful attention was given to the preservation of historical elements to keep the intervention coherent with its original design. This principle also guides the preservation of the stone walls with respect to their original distribution and structure. To gather the sections into one unit, the western section was directly attached to the central section, while the eastern section was connected through a roofed wooden footbridge. This allows for a direct link between the three sections and ground passage between the front and the back of the site. At the eastern section the double slope roof was preserved since it is independent from the other two. Black slate roof tiles integrate the building into the local, cultural, and natural environment. The two main façades perfectly reflect of the climatic conditions they are exposed to, contrasting the northern façade, which is opaque and uniform. Wide, open, and glassed galleries make optimal use of daylight on the south side. The functional structure of the dwelling presents a clear distinction between the private uses on the first floor, and the common use spaces on the ground floor. Accordingly, the first floor houses the bedroom and bathroom in the central and eastern parts, and the kitchen and living room in the western part. Combining the kitchen and living room creates the perfect nexus to place in between the two floors and to spatially seperate their functions.

1

1 The different textures of wood, steel, and stone create a warm and diverse home.

1

2

3

1

ARCHITECT
PLP Atelier

COMPLETION
2020

ORIGINAL BUILDING
19th century

GROSS FLOOR AREA BEFORE | AFTER
260 m² | 260 m²

NUMBER OF ROOMS BEFORE | AFTER
4 | 3

4

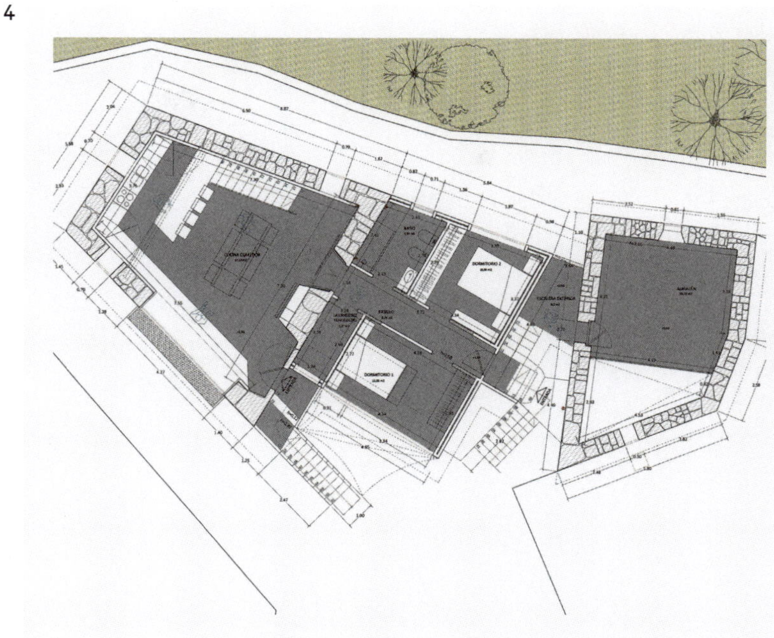

5

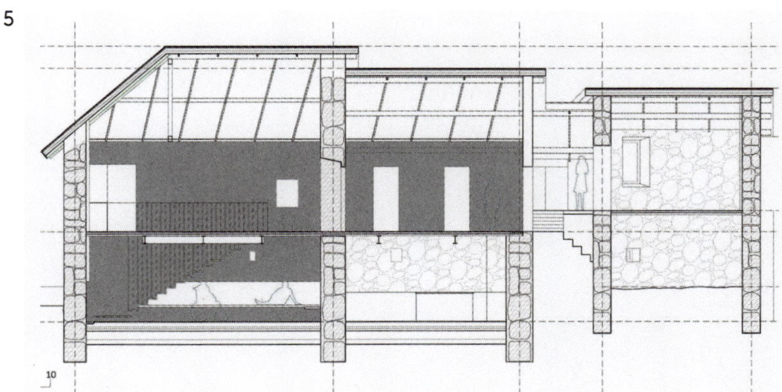

1 A generous skylight transforms this indoor bedroom into an outdoor experience.

2 The newly built footbridge evokes images of the original exterior textures of the building.

3 Coziness and comfort are the main idea in the living room.

4 Ground floor plan

5 Section

São Pedro 27

Sintra, Portugal

The inviting outdoor space is unrecognizable from the ruin it once was.

2

The São Pedro district is part of the city of Sintra, a world heritage village with a mountain full of palaces, castles, and convents in addition to its natural marvels. This house is part of that historic setting but, like so many other unfortunate buildings in Portugal, has been a ruin for decades. Nonetheless the architects believed in its unique location and peculiar features and wanted to renovate it while maintaining the original aspects.

This small building now accommodates two tourist apartments which integrate perfectly into the serene historic neighborhood. Sticking to the original floor plan, the two independent dwellings were kept divided on the ground and first floor. The use of the attic for housing purposes, meant an increase of the height at the middle but still maintained the original height of the edge. Restored and cleaned, the courtyards are a natural outdoor experience in midst of shrubs and trees. Ultimately, the story of the village is reflected in the story of this building – a place with great potential and a history brought to light by this successful renovation.

1

2

3

1 Light fixtures illuminate gloomy corners of the kitchen.

2 The space does not feel restrictive even though it is under the roof slope.

3 A courtyard on each floor allows for easy access to nature.

1

2

3

4

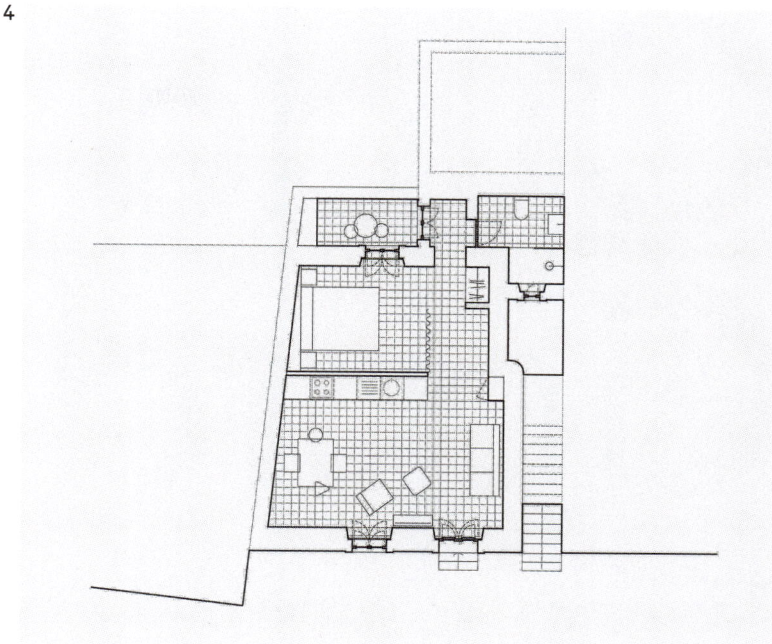

5

2

ARCHITECT
PM-ARQ

COMPLETION
2017

ORIGINAL BUILDING
19th century

GROSS FLOOR AREA BEFORE | AFTER
145 m² | 145 m²

NUMBER OF ROOMS BEFORE | AFTER
4 | 5

1 Turquoise frames accentuate the house front.

2 The sweet pastel colored façade feels infectiously positive.

3 The courtyard functions as an extension of the interior space.

4 Ground floor plan

5 Section

Quad of Gourd

Beijing, China

Reconstructed from scratch, these buildings are a modern reinterpratation of the traditional Chinese neighborhood.

3

Situated in the Luanqing Hutong neighborhood of Beijing, this residence and its small courtyard were in ruins – the roof, doors and windows were so deteriorated they seemingly disappeared. Instead, two large trees have grown inside the house. The goal was to renovate the building as close to the original layout patterns as possible, as they are characteristic for these historic neighborhoods. However, the architects wanted to keep the trees and thus made a few changes to the floor plan.

The courtyard was extended into the structure of the house, splitting the garden into an outer courtyard under the roof and an inner courtyard at the center of the house. To realize the outer court, the roof's structure was repaired using laminated bamboo beams and traditional tiles. Leaving only the area above the trees untiled allows for sufficient sunlight to facilitate their growth. In order to reclaim the space lost to the court expansion, the original living area was expanded through side rooms lined by a continuous vertical grille with series of bamboo screen doors.

The east wing and the southeast corner each contain an apartment including an office in the southwest corner. The bigger west wing functions as a gallery and can be used as an exhibition and event space. The two entrances in the north and south can also be used separately. Skylights bridge the space between the buildings and the curved grille wall. The emerging gourd shape of the garden opens its center to the sky strengthening the Siheyuan spirit while redefining the excessively rigorous spatial order.

Ultimately, this successful intervention helps rebuild the peace of the inner city by creating an introverted utopia to neutralize the bustling outside world. It presents a new model for the regeneration of the old city while transforming the interior into a unique spatial experience.

1

1 The open skylight above the tree allows its unimpeded growth.

1

2

3

3

ARCHITECT
URBANUS

COMPLETION
2017

ORIGINAL BUILDING
Ming Dynasty

GROSS FLOOR AREA BEFORE | AFTER
403 m^2 | 234 m^2

NUMBER OF ROOMS BEFORE | AFTER
3 | 4

4

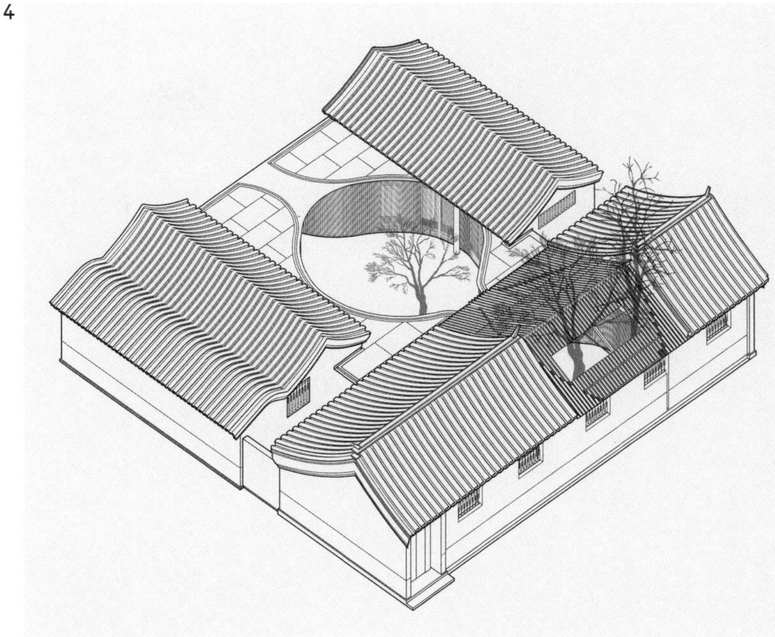

5

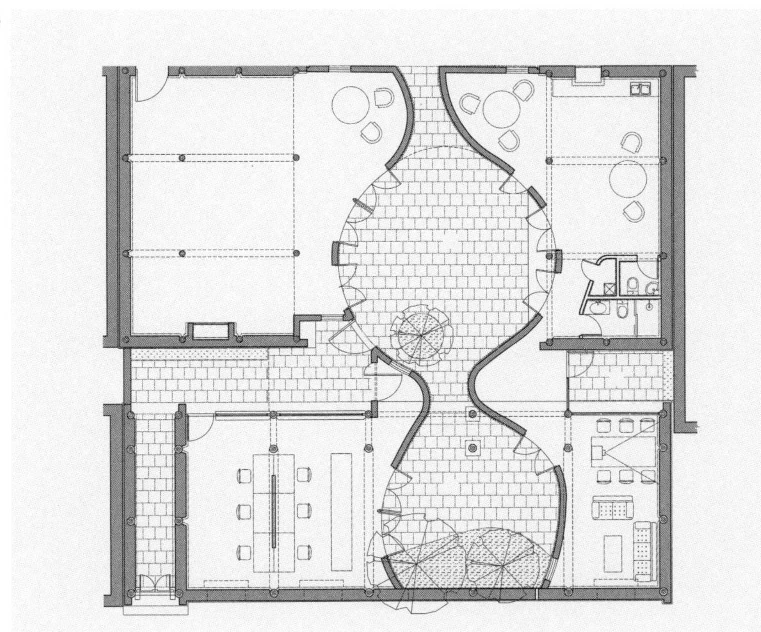

1 The grille walls snake between the buildings gently seperating the spaces.

2 The inner court is the heart of the property.

3 The spacious office has direct access to the outer court.

4 Axonometric projection

5 Ground floor plan

Bamba House

Buenos Aires, Argentina

The balance between contemporary aesthetic and original layout can be adjusted by the new steel envelope.

4

Bamba House is located next to one of the main commercial and vehicular arteries of Buenos Aires, Córdoba Avenue. Once a traditional "chorizo" house from the early 20th century, it has since gone through serial refurbishments that transformed its spatial and material qualities over time.

The aim of this renovation is to reformulate the current condition of the house by building an envelope around it, which mediates between contemporary and original elements. It can be mechanically folded to reveal or conceal different parts of the house and thus offers an endless amount of combinations to change the floor plan and alter its illumination and ventilation. Movement and occupation of space are decided by the residents' needs and can be adjusted to accommodate various occasions.

The infrastructure of the envelope is made of steel while interior surfaces mainly comprise of natural textures such as wood and sheetrock. These are found in the entire room program including the bathroom, kitchen, studio and bedroom. Bright red colored elements such as the decorative door and window frames are an integral part of the interior design and thus highlighted and framed by the contrasting steel structure.

1

2

3

1 A skylight naturally brightens narrow passages in the house.

2 Fully shut, the steel cladding conveys an entirely different ambiance.

3 Clean and simple materials minimize the attention on the envelope itself rather than the effect it produces.

1

2

3

4

ARCHITECT
CCPM Arquitectura

COMPLETION
2019

ORIGINAL BUILDING
1933

GROSS FLOOR AREA BEFORE | AFTER
156 m² | 171 m²

NUMBER OF ROOMS BEFORE | AFTER
6 | 6

4

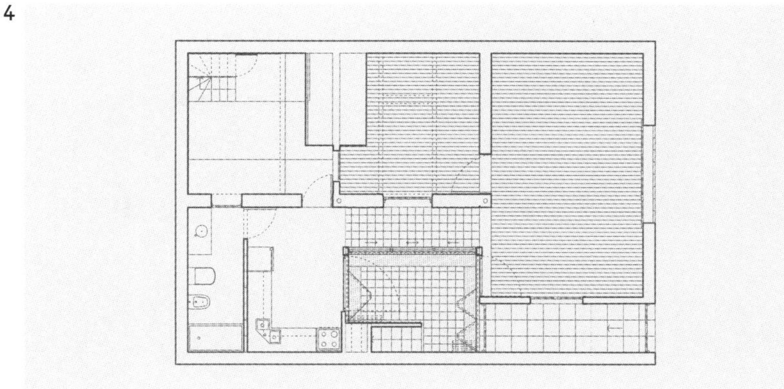

5

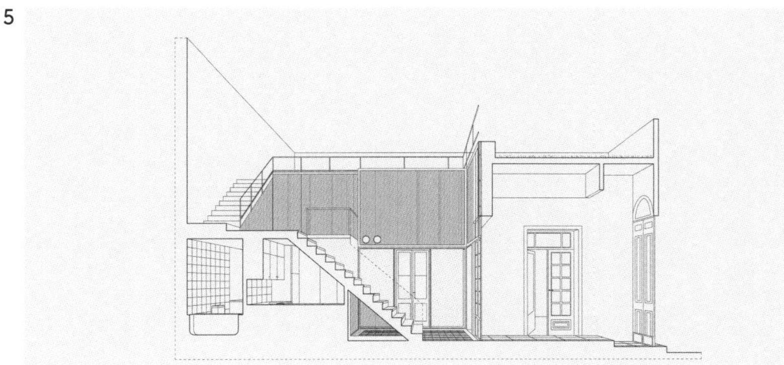

6

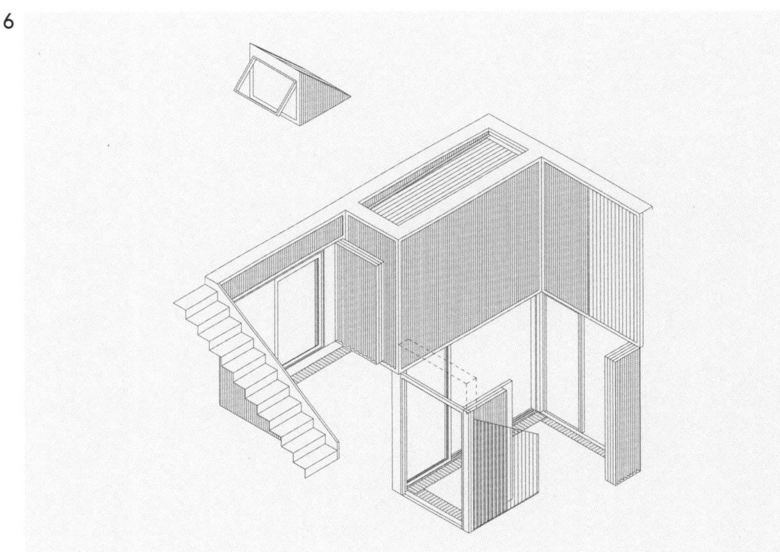

1 The different interior design approaches were carefully matched to harmonize with each other.

2 Red design elements and steel frames are juxtaposed in a direct confrontation.

3 Different angles offer interesting views of the house.

4 Ground floor plan

5 Section with perspective

6 Axonometric projection

House CCB

Valais, Switzerland

Glass walls maintain the stone façade as the highlight of the interior while keeping the exterior design.

5

The massive 1854 building impresses at first glance. It bears the marks of time having evolved from hay barn to stable, and then to wine storage, with a wooden extension added to this family property in 1950. Given its history, one of the most important aspects of this latest renovation was the preservation of the impressive stone façade.

Highlighting the mineral character of the original construction, the architects played with the volumes, giving them a new perspective. A wood and glass cube were carefully placed in the stunning stone shell, turning it into a contemporary living space. The breathtaking view on the freshly brushed timber frame confers to the interior a timeless atmosphere.

From the entrance hall, a concrete staircase leads to the upper floor, with direct access to the main room and the terrace. In perfect balance between two eras, the minimalist allure of the new construction enhances the raw aspect of the old building. The architects used the wooden boards of the old barn to design bespoke furniture for the kitchen and the bedroom, giving new life to the place and the material. In one of the bookshelves, a movable panel unveils an opening between the living room and bathroom to enjoy a relaxing bath with view on the fireplace.

Throughout the day and the year, natural light shapes the space according to the rhythm of nature. In addition to the original narrow windows of the barn, four loopholes are pierced in the roof in order to bring zenithal light in. The subtle lighting was thought down to the smallest detail with the setting sun beautifully filtered by a carved shutter.

1 The wooden extension complements the main building.

2 The stone façade has not been changed for four generations.

3 Inviting, warm light naturally signalizes the entrance area.

1

2

3

1

2

3

4

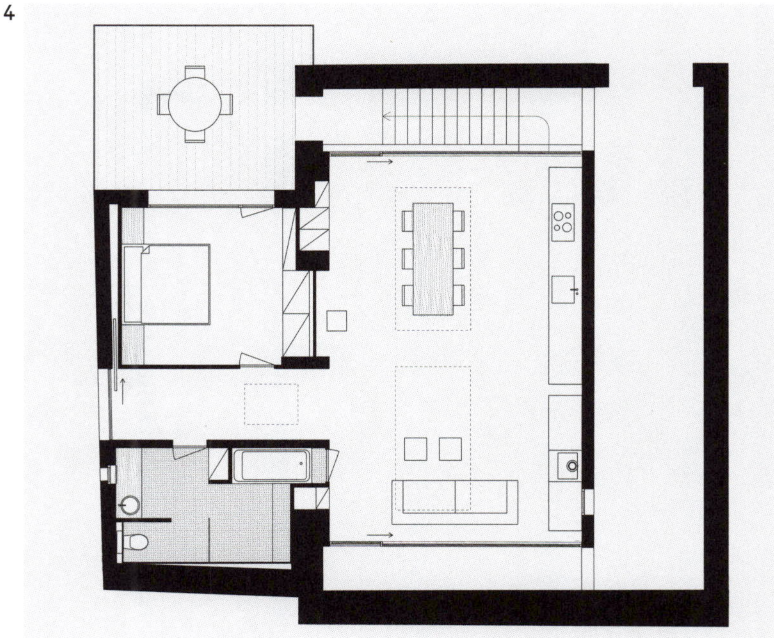

5

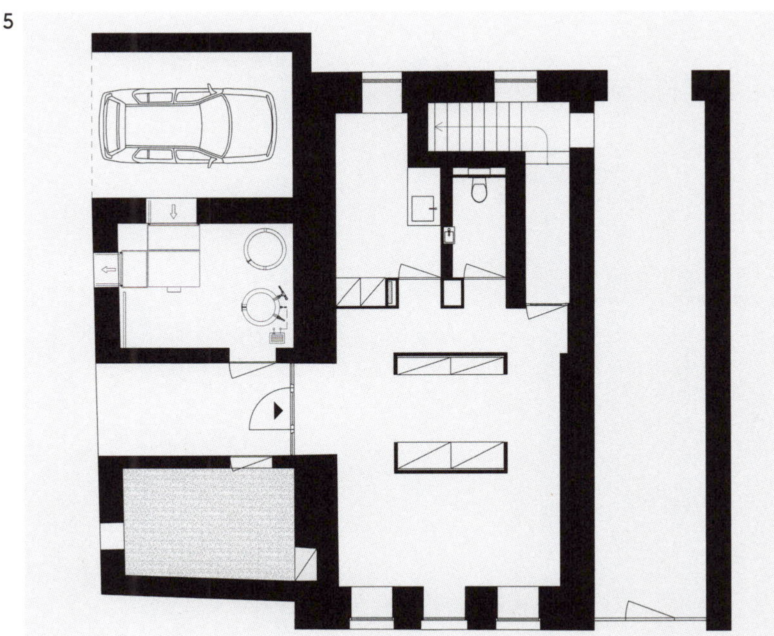

1 The playful light pattern projected through the shutter is reminiscent of floor tiles.

2 The simple color palette reflects the simple bare feel of the stone wall.

3 Texture is a key element in the interior design using mainly natural materials.

4 First floor plan

5 Ground floor plan

5

ARCHITECT
Ralph Germann architectes

COMPLETION
2020

ORIGINAL BUILDING
1854

GROSS FLOOR AREA BEFORE | AFTER
200 m² | 180 m²

NUMBER OF ROOMS BEFORE | AFTER
1 | 5

House Recovery

Černošice, Czech Republic

The worn out house became a cozy home that still matches the rural setting.

6

Above the river in the southern tip of Černošice a worn out building was stabilized and updated. The look of being rooted in the enviroment and arising from the surroundings was preserved. The valley, the proximity of the river and the bridge, the view of the opposite bank, and the rural atmosphere are part of this home. The original task was to transform the weekend ancestral house into a comfortable, all-year-round vacation spot. However, after the construction works were finished, the charms and atmosphere of the place had deeply influenced the builders – who until then lived in an apartment in Prague – that they decided to move in here permanently.

The architects were looking for an efficient use of the existing floor plan with minimal interventions. They used original elements and surfaces with all traces of their history: The magic of the wear and tear had to be preserved. The original layout of the ground floor was mirrored so that the living room and kitchen face the garden. From the garden a new entrance to the previously unused attic and a new staircase were created. The space beneath the staircase is used as a pantry with two bedrooms and a bathroom in the attic. The backyard is still at the stage of transformation. The house reflects complexity of different natures, tastes and interests of its inhabitants.

1

2

1 The minimalism of modern windows and doors perfectly match the simplicity of rural structures.

2 New stairs are situated between historic walls.

1

2

3

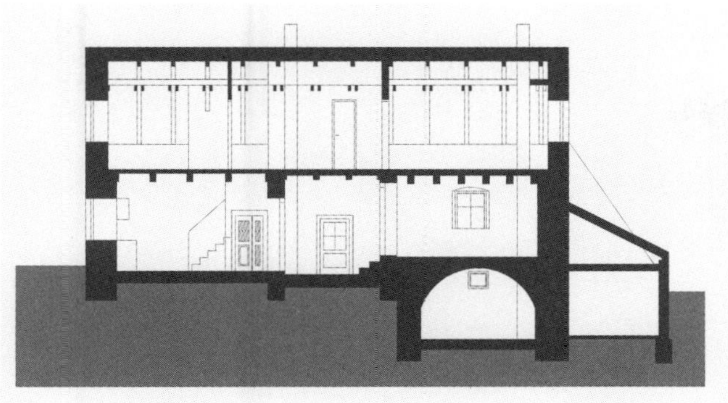

4

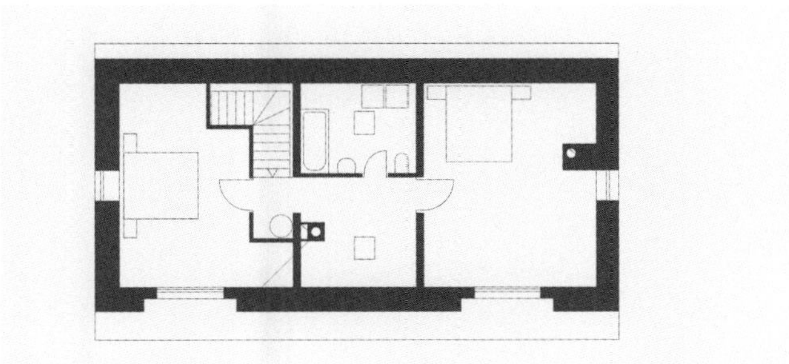

5

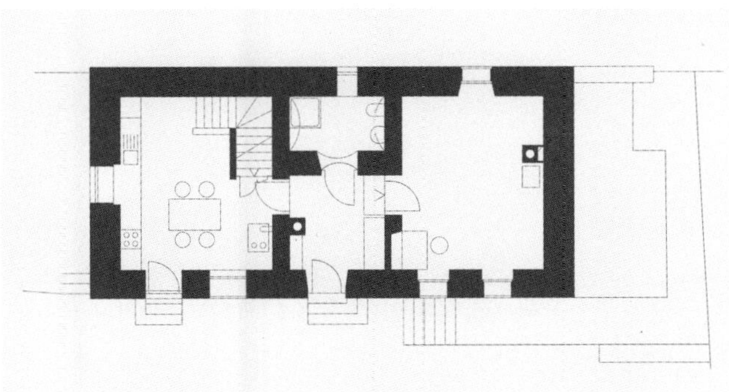

6

ARCHITECT
3+1 architekti

COMPLETION
2018

ORIGINAL BUILDING
around 1900

GROSS FLOOR AREA BEFORE | AFTER
115 m² | 115 m²

NUMBER OF ROOMS BEFORE | AFTER
4 | 3

1 A new beam ceiling was constructed in the kitchen on the ground floor.

2 The ceiling was resaturated in the living room on the ground floor.

3 Section

4 First floor plan

5 Ground floor plan

House Minard

Ghent, Belgium

The new architecture of House Minard exists in symbiosis with the historical construction.

7

Designed in 1851 by the Ghent architect Louis Minard, House Minard provides the canvas for the clients' wishes: a space to live, work and relax in the heart of the city. The original house has generous hallways and saloons. The contrast between a wide and light, decorated staircase with curved lines and its narrow, dark opponent with straight lines tells the story of the double life that used to take place in the house: the owner on the one, the staff on the other hand. Before its transformation, a new extension that was built against the rear wall separated the historical spaces from the courtyard, darkening them. The demolition of the extension leads to a radical new interpretation of the house: living in the basement, working on the ground floor, sleeping on the first and second floors, a studio and workplace in the attic and fitness in the new rear house. The basement was given a major upgrade to kitchen and living space. By deepening the cellars, a kitchen with abundant natural light and a strong connection to the garden is created. The historical corridors and saloons were restored to their former glory.

1

2

3

4

1 The curved staircase connects the different levels.

2 Some elements remain their patina, which creates an unique and luxurious atmosphere.

3 Ground floor plan

4 The dining area has an open view over the garden.

7

ARCHITECT
aNNo architecten

COMPLETION
2017

ORIGINAL BUILDING
1851

GROSS FLOOR AREA BEFORE | AFTER
895 m² | 830 m²

NUMBER OF ROOMS BEFORE | AFTER
24 | 20

Old Concrete House

Stara Zagora, Bulgaria

Cleared of all plants, the intricate details of the house façade can be appreciated again.

8

Prior to its reconstruction, this house from the 1920s was a romantic, rather isolated ruin, surrounded by authentic fragments of the ancient city of Augusta Traiana, and new-built elements from the contemporary city. The intervention bridges the time that has since passed and evolves the design of the house into an avant-garde contemporary interpretation of itself.

A new volume of white concrete complements the structure of the old house by extending its back. The composition of the openings, the materiality and the ambiguous elements of the annex blend the two entities while their layout preserves the historic view of the façade. The new winding designer staircase and its translucent steps bring light into the center of the entire building. New glossy white concrete slabs integrate and conceal all of the contemporary technology of the house. The interior has been updated as well, with modern flair and simple colors dominating the new living space.

1

2

3

1 Light cascades down the hypnotizing staircase.

2 Dark wood and black finishes suit the grounding simplistic interior.

3 Glass panels as room dividers open the space while seperating the different functions.

1

2

3

8

ARCHITECT
I/O architects

COMPLETION
2017

ORIGINAL BUILDING
1920s

GROSS FLOOR AREA BEFORE | AFTER
405 m² | 425 m²

NUMBER OF ROOMS BEFORE | AFTER
13 | 10

4

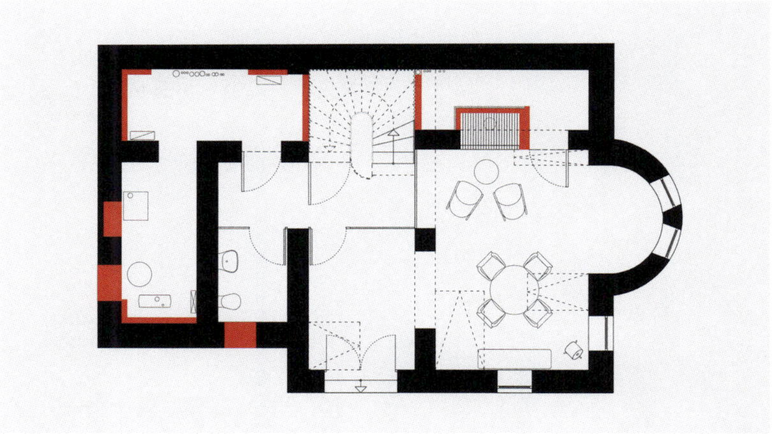

5

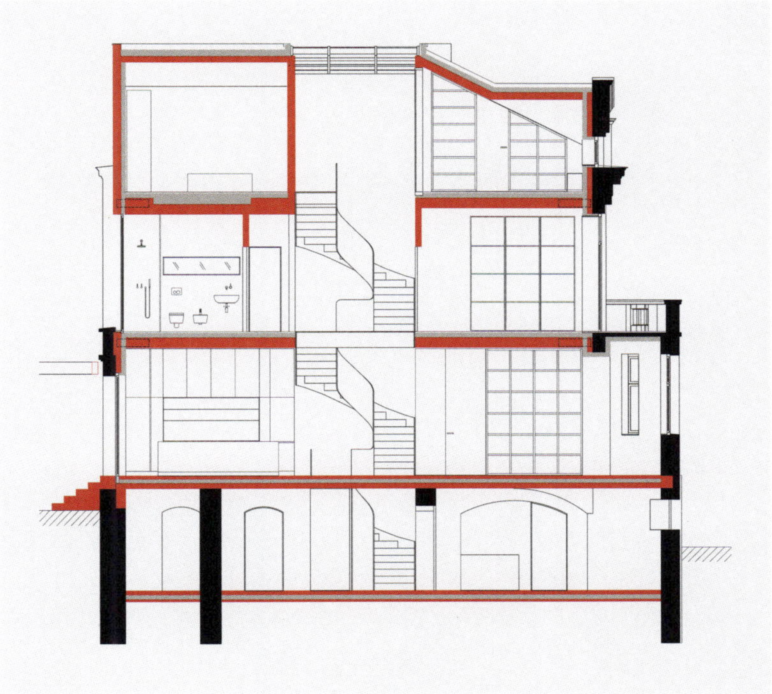

1 Remnants of historic pillars and masonry surround the building.

2 The annex distinguishes itself from the original building through its angular form.

3 The patio in the back includes an outdoor kitchen area.

4 Ground floor plan

5 Section

Rural House in Pontemieiro

Vale de Cambra, Portugal

The white façade clearly shows the renovation of this house.

9

The village of Pontemieiro is located to the west of Vale de Cambra, in midst of dispersed settlements that characterize this territory. This small house stands out from a group of old buildings that have been restored, contributing to the recovery and revitalization of the village. It was in an advanced state of degradation but some remnants of the materials, colors, and details were evident, such as traces of an old whitewashed façade, the exterior frame details, and the wooden roof structure.

Aiming to establish a sense of continuity with the past, the architects took great care to respect the dynamics of the building's original structure and its respective materials without, however, reproducing its initial design in detail. Therefore, a reinterpretation was proposed to adapt rural construction traditions to contemporary lifestyle.

The available space on the upper floor was transformed while preserving the open floor plan of the layout. Sanitary devices and a folding bed are integrated into a functional cubic volume hence allowing for informal use of the generous room surrounding it. On the lower floor, the existing space was reclaimed and converted into a multipurpose room that complements the upper main space. The characteristic stone façade was revitalized in a fresh coat of white paint, which still allows the raw texture of the wall to shine through. The old broken wooden doors were replaced with new teal colored doors, which match the color of the kitchen furniture and blend nicely with the overall natural color palette and the wooden interior design.

1

1 The functional cube is kept low-key, withdrawn to one side of the room.

1

2

3

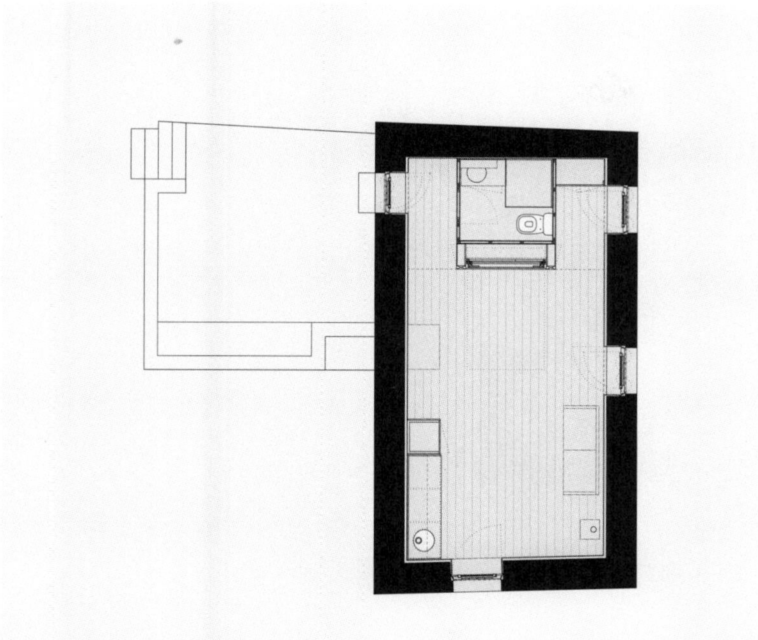

4

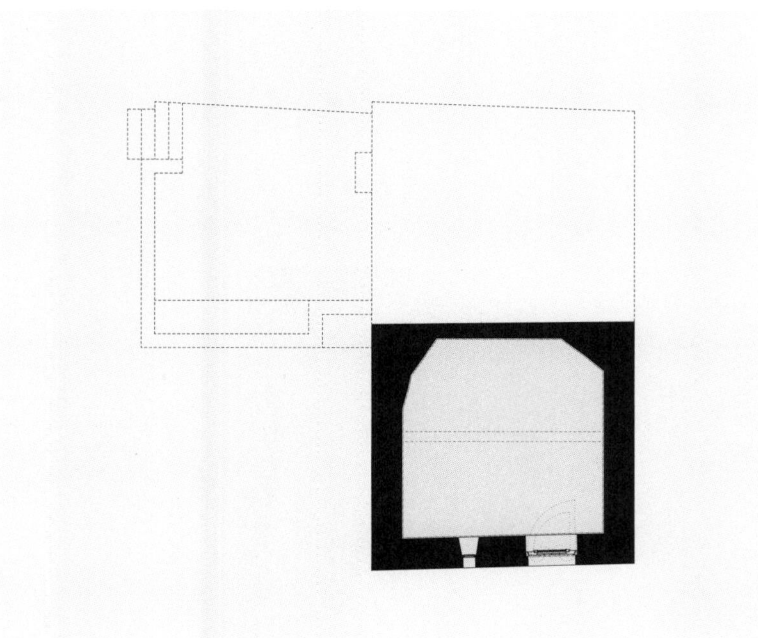

9

ARCHITECT
André Eduardo Tavares Arquitecto

COMPLETION
2018

ORIGINAL BUILDING
1850

GROSS FLOOR AREA BEFORE | AFTER
60 m² | 60 m²

NUMBER OF ROOMS BEFORE | AFTER
2 | 3

1 Furniture is kept to the walls leaving multifunctional space at the center.

2 A simple color palette visually declutters the space.

3 Upper floor plan

4 Lower floor plan

Conversion House Ca

Ascona, Switzerland

Reduced to a simple stone cube, the newly rebuilt house is interwoven with the old garden walls and forms a grown unit with the old garden.

10

The existing house to be rebuilt is located in an interesting urban location, closely connected to the historic village center of Ascona, which is accessible by car and on foot. It has a romantic palm garden and an unobstructed view of the roofs of the village center, Lake Maggiore, and the mountains. Due to its steep slope, the neighborhood on Via Rondonico is strongly characterized by high retaining walls, which are generally built in traditional natural stone masonry. The existing house makes no reference to the architecture of the site but its relationship to the garden and the garden itself have a special quality.

The conversion project responds to the site and the terraced garden with its stone walls. Natural stone walls as exterior cladding and as walls in the interior living space, with traditional Rasapietra plastering – half plastering combined with fully plastered walls – give the house a new and site-specific identity while allowing it to fit naturally into the garden and the neighborhood.

The existing natural stone retaining wall along the valley-side street was partially demolished to create a new generous entrance situation. Behind the remaining wall, an additional technical, vehicle, and storage room was integrated below the ground level. From the garden gate at the parking lot, a gently rising ramp leads to the lower existing garden level, where the garden stairs and natural stone walls can be largely preserved and used for access to the two building floors. Reduced to a simple stone cube, the rebuilt house is interwoven with the old garden walls and forms a grown unit with the old garden.

1

2

1 The spacious living, dining, and cooking hall opens to the valley side with an over-corner full glazing.

2 The new entrance area receives a modern look through the use of glass.

1

2

10

ARCHITECT
Wespi de Meuron Romeo Architekten

COMPLETION
2017

ORIGINAL BUILDING
1950s

GROSS FLOOR AREA BEFORE | AFTER
140 m² | 180 m²

NUMBER OF ROOMS BEFORE | AFTER
3 ½ | 4 ½

3

4

1 The natural stone walls are not only used as an exterior cladding but also for the interior walls.

2 The upper floor bedroom is characterized by a mix of natural materials and colors.

3 Ground floor plan

4 Second floor plan

1960s Remodeling

Meerbusch, Germany

The extension fuses the once seemingly separate buildings into one.

11

The property is located on a corner plot in Meerbusch, bordering a residential street to the east and north. Originally, the building was an office with residential units and garages.

The 1960s Remodeling was a conversion and core renovation of the building in massive construction. In favor of valuable exterior space and a clear building structure, the annexes and garage were dismantled. What remained were the cubes, which are characterized by their L-configuration, clear geometry and their different façade materials. In keeping with the architectural language of the 1960s, the longer single-story structure was again emphasized as the horizontal and the two-story structure as the vertical. Additionally, space had to be gained to meet the demands of a family.

In order to not only emphasize the existing room geometries, but also to make optimal use of them, they were extended by a single-story wing from north to south, at the intersection of the L-legs. This allowed the desired merging of the entrance, dining and living areas as well as the kitchen into one spacious complex. The private living spaces, on the other hand, are clearly partitioned to the east in the two-story building. Gained space allowed the entrance to be relocated from the north to the east along with a new staircase. As part of the core renovation, the entire building infrastructure was brought up to the latest standards.

1

2

1 The entrance is redefined by the big open entrance area.

2 Although the façade of each cube is made of different materials, they are visually connected by their white color.

1

2

11

ARCHITECT
E2architekten

COMPLETION
2017

ORIGINAL BUILDING
1963, Manfred Wehnert

GROSS FLOOR AREA BEFORE | AFTER
507 m² | 551 m²

NUMBER OF ROOMS BEFORE | AFTER
23 | 27

3

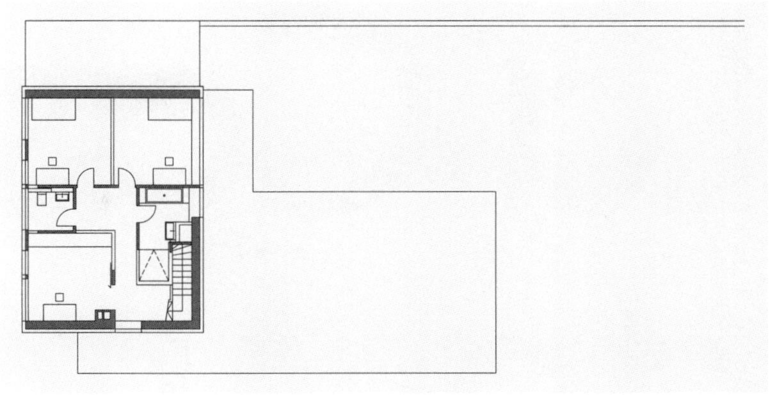

4

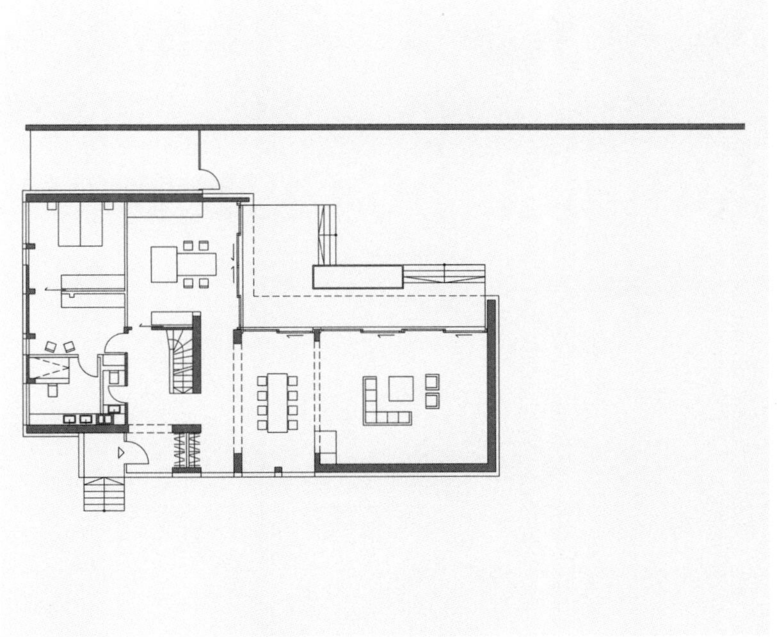

1 The basic idea of two volumes differentiated by their geometry is clearly visible.

2 The extension allows the patio to be accessed via the kitchen.

3 First floor plan

4 Ground floor plan

La Casa del Ángel

Jumilla, Spain

Nestled into the landscape, this eye-catching brick hut feels right at home in nature.

12

This country refuge is located in the Sierra de Jumilla and has supported the passage of hikers, hunters and mountaineers for decades. Given its relevance to its environment, both geographically and socially, the works on this small building were far more than a mere architectural intervention. The landscape value of this delicate refuge meant that the architects needed to pay special attention to both the existing architecture and the landscape surrounding it.

The aim of the restoration is to open the shelter to the surroundings, to the landscape, to the mountain range. Therefore, apart from maintaining and renewing the interior, the project also involved the outdoor space. Shade, nooks, and benches for all kinds of passers-by were provided, making the shelter a landscape piece that can be used from both the inside and outside. The effective interior space arrangement accompanied by the improvement of thermal and acoustic isolation transforms this refuge into a suitable place to rest and relax. In addition, the wood used for the structure, windows and doors compliment the original masonry giving the entire space a warm atmosphere. Replacing the original roof with a concrete one provides proper isolation to the inside space and shade to the outdoor space. Walls are covered with various reddish brickwork – a stark contrast to the intense green of the landscape in which the hut stands out. None of the materials are coated, taking advantage of its bareness to attract other kinds of inhabitants like plants, insects, birds and many more. As a result, it is a sustainable, recognizable and integrated building that is part of the landscape to which it belongs.

1 The bright colored bricks charm onlookers even though the interior itself is quite minimal.

1

1

2

3

3

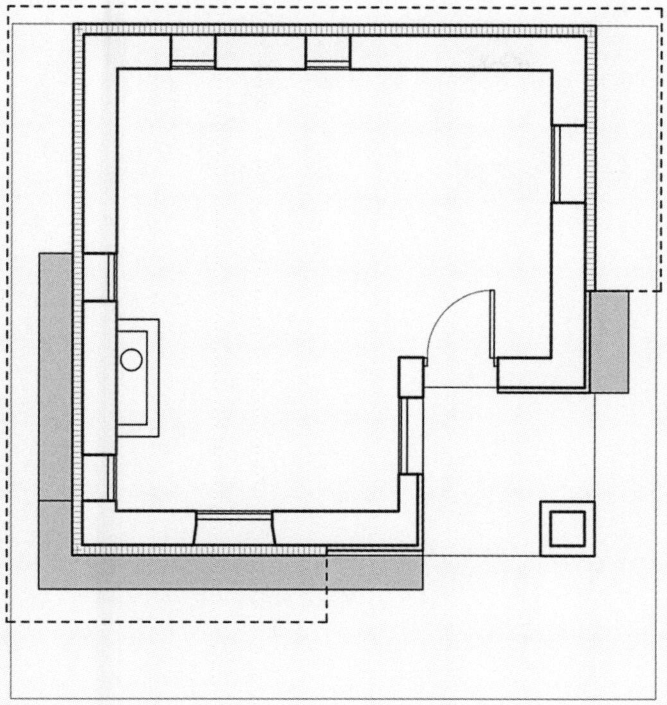

12

ARCHITECT
MARTIN LEJARRAGA

COMPLETION
2018

ORIGINAL BUILDING
1962

GROSS FLOOR AREA BEFORE | AFTER
35 m² | 38 m²

NUMBER OF ROOMS BEFORE | AFTER
4 | 1

1 Many different bricks make up the interesting visual of the walls.

2 Clearly defined lines distinguish the hut from its enviroment.

3 A concrete bench wraps all the way around the building.

Casa Alonso

Zaragoza, Spain

The once oppressively tight house is now open and inviting.

13

This project is situated in a typical working-class neighborhood of Zaragoza and was built in the second half of the last century. The small house was regenerated and transformed for new owners without losing the essence of its initial identity. Prior to the intervention, the single-story dwelling was understood as a very tight container along the road, squeezed between the adjacent houes. It was compartmentalized in three bays perpendicular to the façade, including a garden in the backyard. After the intervention, the spaces are reconfigured in respect to the three bays but also to accommodate contemporary lifestyle. The technical architect was Pablo Sebastián, who collaborated with Alejandro Alda.

The first bay gathers the entrance, kitchen and dining area and expands the space outwards by accessing the rear garden through big glass doors. This allows for a visually rich and functional relationship of the interior space and the garden. The living room, the heart of the house, is in the second bay, placed between the rest of the rooms. It functions as a link to turn the rooms around it into one open space. Bedroom and dressing room, the most private areas of the house, are located in the third bay, with the bathroom as a central piece. The sink and shower are divided into two spaces, each having their own differentiated area. Separating these two spaces enables residents to use the sanitary devices independently without disturbing one another.

1 Even though it is one open space, each area has its distinct purpose.

2 A limited color palette unifies each functional area for one consistent interior style.

1

2

1

2

3

13

ARCHITECT
Sebastián Arquitectos
with
Iván Paul Martín Jefremovas

COMPLETION
2019

ORIGINAL BUILDING
1949, José Beltran

GROSS FLOOR AREA BEFORE | AFTER
84,40 m² | 84,40 m²

NUMBER OF ROOMS BEFORE | AFTER
3 | 1

4

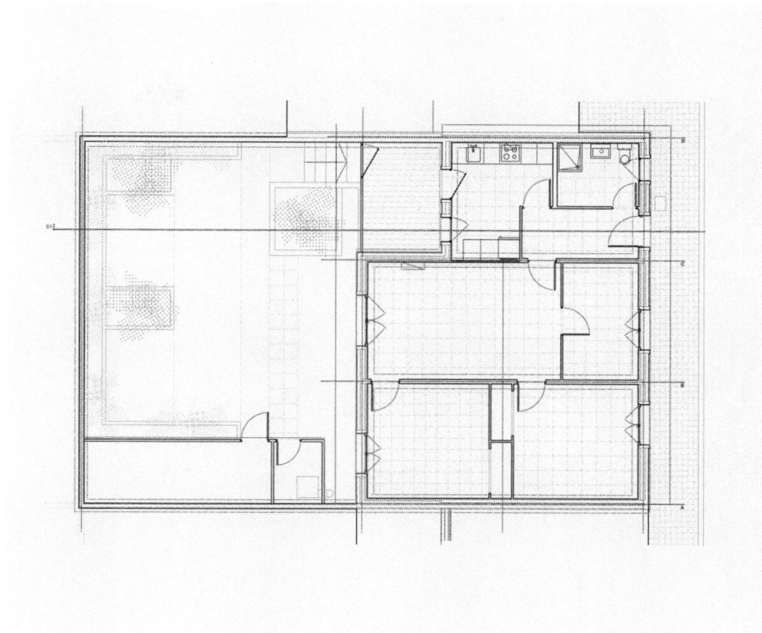

5

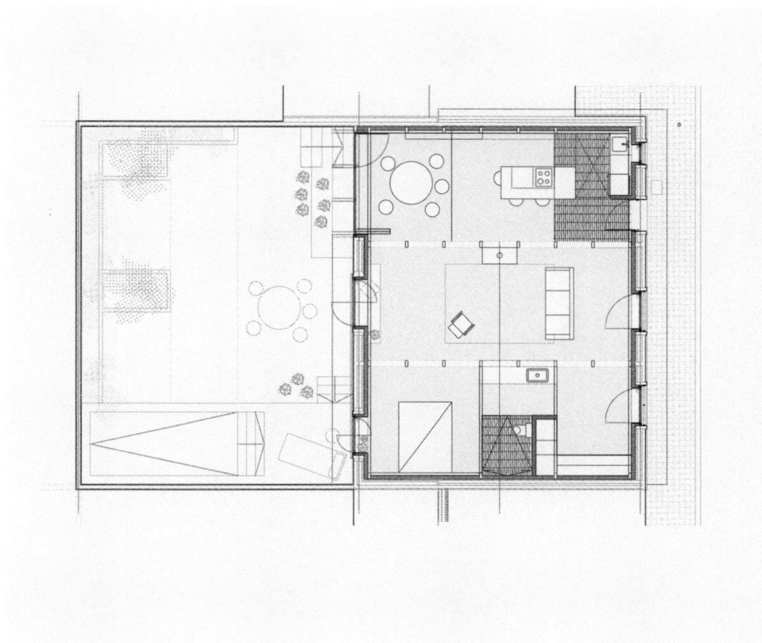

1 The ladder to the upper floor bed room also works as a towel rack.

2 The bathroom and bedroom floor are seamlessly level.

3 Al rooms function together as one open continuous space.

4 Ground floor plan before

5 Ground floor plan after

Haarlem House

Haarlem, The Netherlands

The wedge-shaped extension is clad with ribs and planks to create depth in the façade.

14

The original layout of the three-story house was characterized by a narrow service bay and a wide bay including the living and dining room. The two sections were connected by a small door-way. The house is now completely refurbished and expanded, including the top floor and roof terrace. Additional space for the kitchen and a sunny terrace in the garden is provided by the angled rear façade of the extension. The ground floor plan is conceived as a collection of rooms with different sizes and shapes.

Large openings enable free circulation around the rooms and continuously change the viewer's perspective. The flooring divides the former service and living area using colored tiling in the hall and kitchen and aged timber planks in the other rooms. Clad with charred wood in a pattern of ribs and planks, and finished with an aged copper coping, the façade is kept understated. A timber folding door connects the garden to the terrace, while a fixed window provides an open view through the house as well as its kitchen, all the way to the other side.

1

2

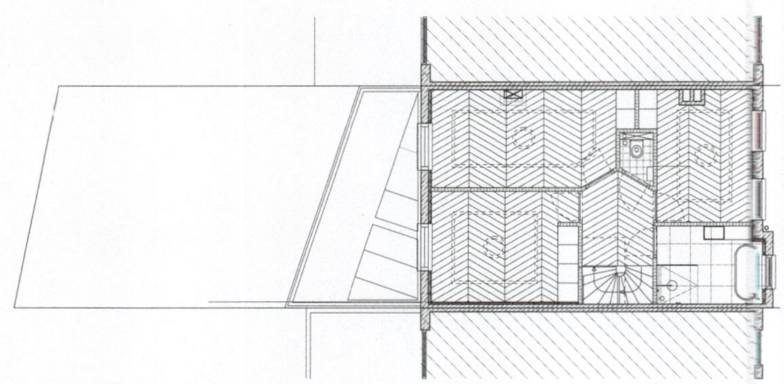

3

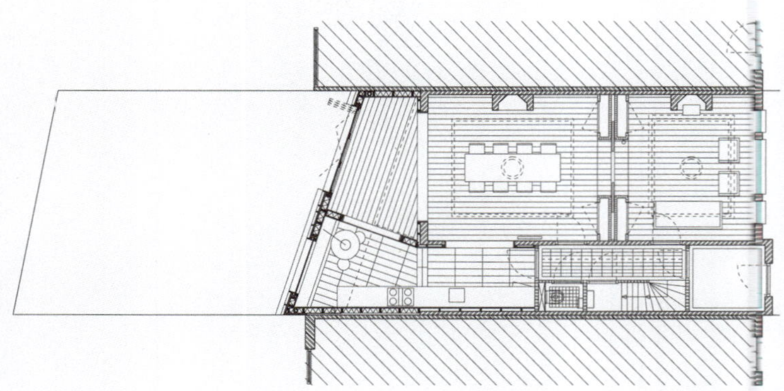

4

1 The simple interior of timber and off-white plaster visually merges with the outside.

2 First floor plan

3 Ground floor plan

4 The ground floor has bright and open spaces after its refurbishment.

14

ARCHITECT
Unknown Architects

COMPLETION
2021

ORIGINAL BUILDING
1905

GROSS FLOOR AREA BEFORE | AFTER
135 m² | 186 m²

NUMBER OF ROOMS BEFORE | AFTER
9 | 11

Residence at Lerchenberg

Durlach, Germany

The remodeled house is worlds apart from its historic predecessor.

15

This project is a small house from the 1960s in a prime residential area of Karlsruhe. The house was in a substandard condition: dark, narrow, winding, and worn out. Nevertheless, the location is good, the property is large, the split level is interesting due to the slope. There were many possibilities for change in the remodeling design. With just a few changes, the interior of the house was transformed into a fascinating floor plan - small, but expandable due to the sloping floor. The former basement level now serves as an entry level with the children's bedrooms. The previously gloomy living room is now a spacious, light-flooded kitchen with a dining area in front of the fireplace. Consequent restriction to only a few materials such as white plaster and oak wood, gives the actually modest rooms their generous spaciousness. These factors combined with the magnificent plot give the house the impression of a Nordic summer house.

1

2

3

1 A big glass window extends the kitchen into the garden.

2 The combination of white plaster and wood results in a clean yet warm environment.

3 The house can also be accessed via the kitchen.

1

2

3

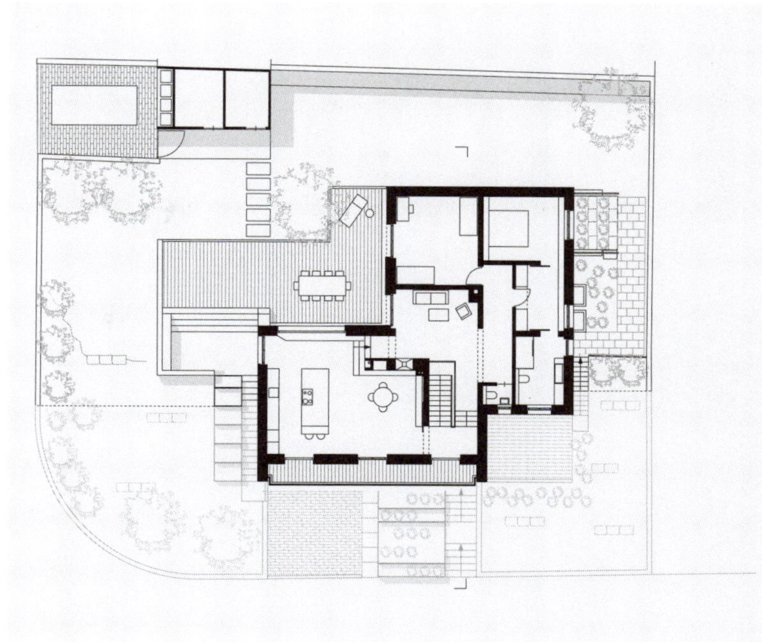

4

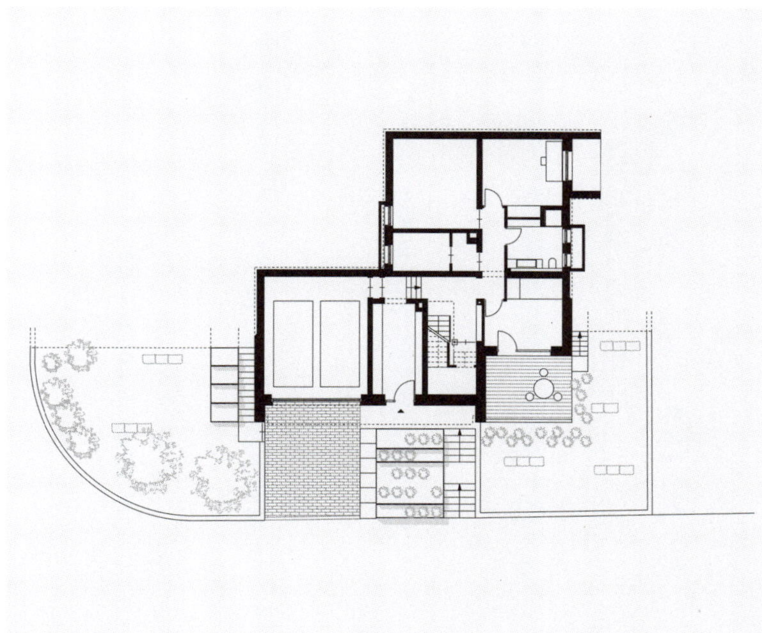

1 The clutter-free interior connects seamlessly to the outside area.

2 The kitchen and dining area function as one space.

3 Ground floor plan

4 Basement level plan

15

ARCHITECT
baurmann.dürr Architekten

COMPLETION
2020

ORIGINAL BUILDING
1962, Alois Schneider

GROSS FLOOR AREA BEFORE | AFTER
312 m² | 312 m²

NUMBER OF ROOMS BEFORE | AFTER
5 | 6

Toon & Ina

Ghent, Belgium

The charming row of house fronts lives on undisturbed owing to the mindful restoration of this building.

16

5

When the architects took on this building in the center of Ghent, they were faced with a complex renovation project to create one contemporary family home from two connected historic buildings. The volumes have been preserved almost everywhere. However, it was impossible to restore authentically because the buildings had already been renovated many times over their 600-year life. The buildings, mostly dating back to 1620, and the basement, a former wine cellar from the 14th century, needed to be turned into one cohesive unit while still respecting their history.

To establish the link between all levels of the two buildings, a complex with wooden stairs was developed in the shaft. These allow circulation between the floors in both parts. This stair complex between the historic buildings allows for light to reach deep into the house through the original roof truss. Downstairs the playful padouk stairwell is reminiscent of an M. C. Escher drawing. The rock garden patio constitutes an ambiguous inside and outside space with the slate-paved floor enhancing the effect. The massive wooden trusses and the original ceilings were kept, while the floors above were reconstructed. Both, the new floors and any other customizations, are made of oak – iconic for this project. A new tube-shaped service wing, integrated in the inner garden, carries the elevator, bathrooms and toilets, the electricity and all other utilities on every floor without disturbing the house. Except for some retouching, the hall remained untouched with plastering and painting very carefully done only where necessary to make the form of the house legible again.

1 The geometrical stairs create an interesting spacial experience.

1

1

2

3

16

ARCHITECT
atelier vens vanbelle

COMPLETION
2018

ORIGINAL BUILDING
1340, 1620

GROSS FLOOR AREA BEFORE | AFTER
499 m² | 496 m²

NUMBER OF ROOMS BEFORE | AFTER
17 | 17

4

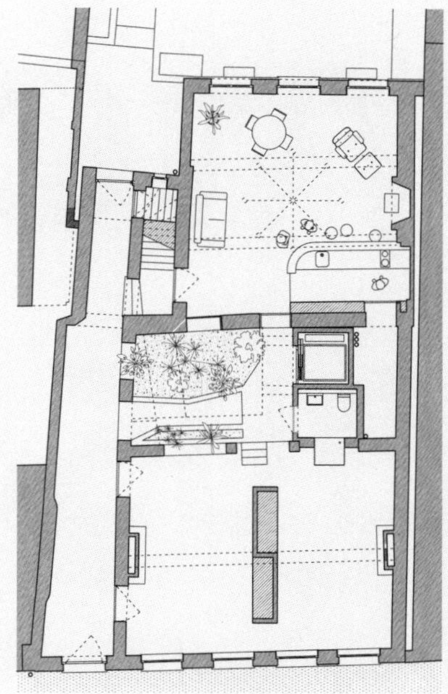

5

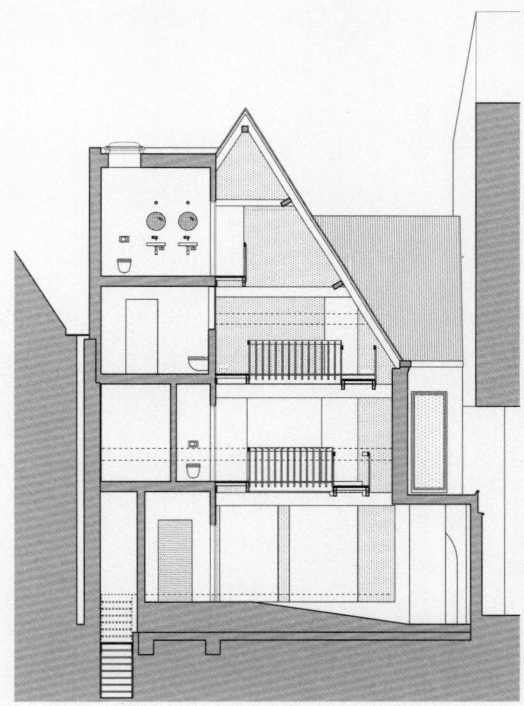

1 Rooms are directly connected through the network of stairs.

2 Wooden ceiling trusses enrich the space with more texture.

3 The original structure of the house remains part of the interior design.

4 Ground floor plan

5 Section

Plywood House

Palma de Mallorca, Spain

Bright tiles and vivid color accents are integral to the revitalization of this house.

17

11

This project, located in a quiet neighborhood of Palma de Mallorca, has been approached as two parallel lines of research. The architects wanted to explore the possibilities of local manufacturing of plywood elements while also conducting a deep study on the crafts still alive on the island.

The original house needed to be expanded with an additional floor while not overloading the original stone walls. Thus, a lightweight structure of 244 by 122 centimeter poplar plywood boards was built off-site, which allowed necessary further testing because of its high dependance on the manufacturing process. The optimization of CNC routing and the structural requirements generated an interesting geometric pattern that can be replicated in other buildings. The plywood structure is bare and uncoated, showing the building's design of the ceiling. Primary materials like wood, stone or terracotta are used in their raw state with ornaments decorating the interior. These are made by local artisans using local materials with different degrees of industrialization. Floor tiles from companies like Huguet, which have manufactured concrete tiles in Mallorca for decades, and special terracotta tiles from Miquel Soler, a traditional manufacturer from Felanitx, have been used on several parts of the façade and pool.

Various ambiences establish themselves inside the house using diffused light, extended indoor-to-outdoor spaces, and views of the nearby Castle in the afternoon sun. Different parts of the house have consciously been designed to include more or less thermal insulation allowing for seasonal migration inside the home. With only wet rooms and kitchen having a fixed purpose, the remaining interior space stays adaptable to the residents' needs, transforming the home into a diverse atmospheric experience.

1

1 The layout of the tiles and the angular design of the ceiling create a natural ensemble.

1

2

3

4

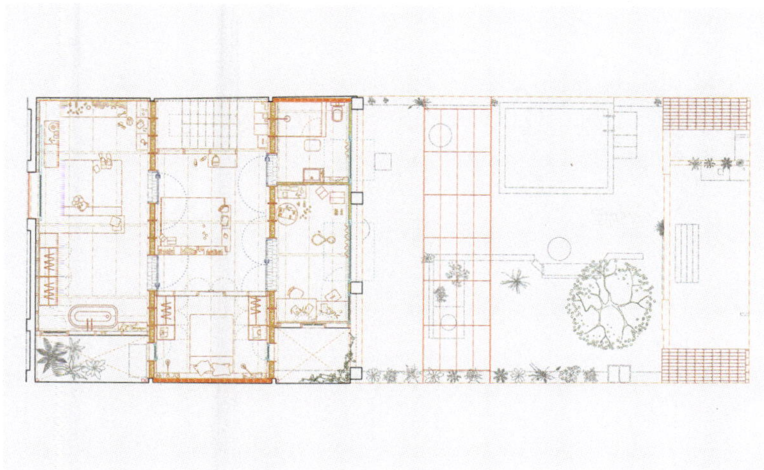

5

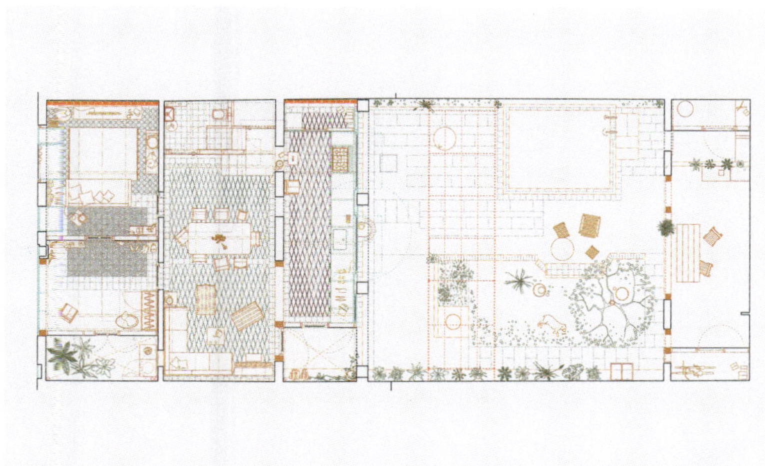

17

ARCHITECT
Feina Studio

COMPLETION
2016

ORIGINAL BUILDING
1920

GROSS FLOOR AREA BEFORE | AFTER
115 m² | 200 m²

NUMBER OF ROOMS BEFORE | AFTER
2 | 3

1 Different floor tiles seperate the functional spaces of the house.

2 Natural materials such as clay, wood and stone are reflected in the outside space.

3 The natural light-colored plywood texture warms the simplistic stair design.

4 First floor plan

5 Ground floor plan

Old Town House S

Rothenburg ob der Tauber, Germany

The spectacular view of and from the house is a big part of the exterior and interior design.

18

A space for young and modern living in midst historic surroundings was created in the center of Rothenburg ob der Tauber's old town. The concept of the Old Town House S combines old and new in a perfect combination of renovation of an existing building and extension by an annex.

The interior implements the concept harmoniously in a juxta position of existing walls and fine, high-quality interior plaster. The synthesis of old and new thus moved from the outside to the inside and creates a modern living space in a unique environment. It is particularly distinct through the main features of the remodeled and supplemented architecture: Modern steel staircases and a light-flooded glass box form a counterpoint to the old town, which is characterized by punched windows and dark rooms. Situated directly on the historic city wall, the building offers its residents a breathtaking view over the Tauber valley.

1

2

3

1 Modern interior design choices appropriately contrast the historic masonry.

2 The glassed fireplace is embedded into the wall.

3 The existing brick wall is on showcase in the hallway.

1

2

3

18

ARCHITECT
architekturstudio SCHROTH

LIGHTING DESIGN
Lichtraum, Würzburg

COMPLETION
2021

ORIGINAL BUILDING
1907, Gebrüder Unbehauen
1920, Johann Stellmag
1956, Ernst Deuther

GROSS FLOOR AREA BEFORE | AFTER
243 m² | 476 m²

NUMBER OF ROOMS BEFORE | AFTER
15 | 17

4

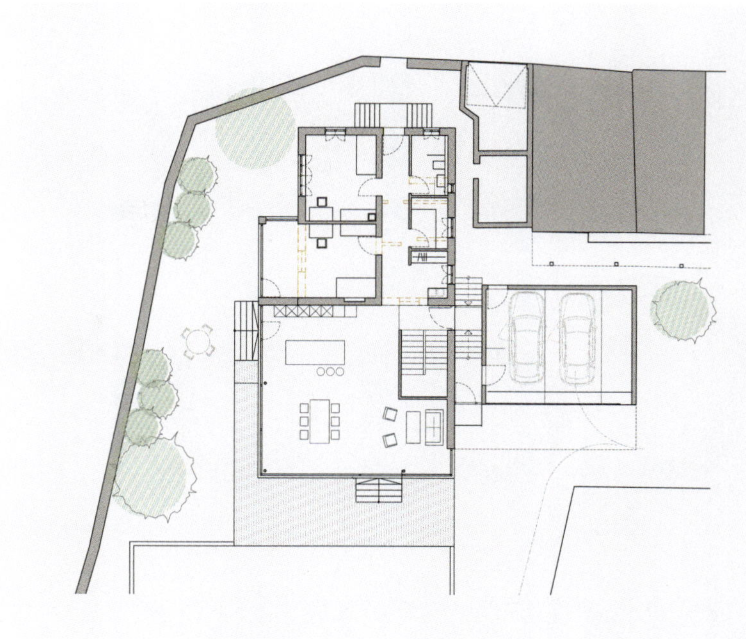

5

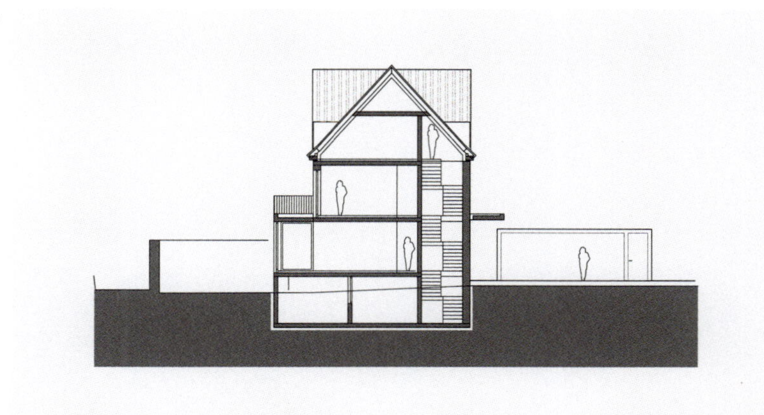

1 The different textures of the walls, floor, and furniture are well matched.

2 White walls, open windows, and a big mirror brighten up the bathroom.

3 The scenic view of the landscape is framed and exhibited throughout the interior.

4 Ground floor plan

5 Section

Moradia Caramão

Lisboa, Portugal

The refurbishment of this house revitalizes it and puts it in context with the surrounding neighborhood.

19

The existing plot consisted of a garden on three fronts of a house that was aesthetically disjointed from its neighborhood, characterized by originally simple and austere houses. Intended as a family home, the project's main purposes were to recover the image of the existing house and to expand it by adding a new volume with a different formal and spatial language.

The front door once repellent was redefined and is now clean and inviting. Interior layouts were completely reorganized, and the roof's morphology was adjusted to accommodate for a new attic. The front façade was fully maintained, while the view on the sides and back of the house were altered by the integration of the new volume. New solar oriented windows on the north, south, and west side guide light into the building to create a more open and spacious feeling home. In the backyard, a swimming pool and an exterior dining area were added.

1

2

3

1 Big windows extend the space outwards to the surroundings.

2 The floor-length window corner acts as an entrance to the garden.

3 The pool is attached to the side of the house and matches its color and material.

1

2

3

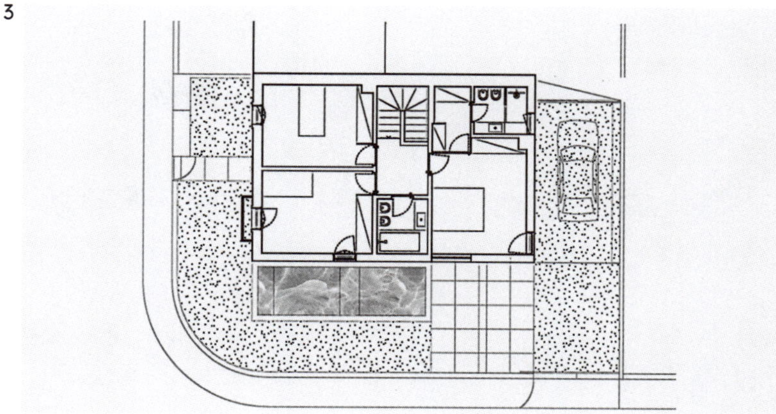

4

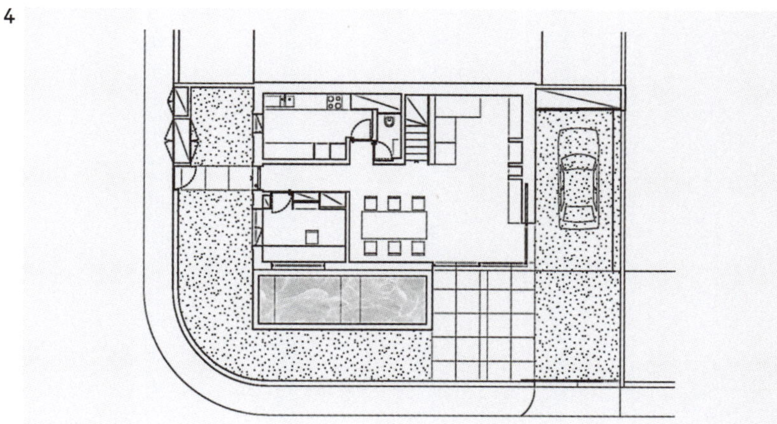

5

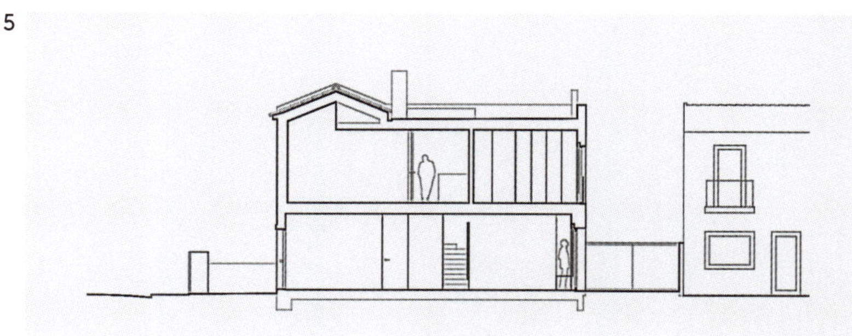

19

ARCHITECT
Atelier Cais

COMPLETION
2020

ORIGINAL BUILDING
1940s

GROSS FLOOR AREA BEFORE | AFTER
75 m² | 150 m²

NUMBER OF ROOMS BEFORE | AFTER
4 | 3

1 The west façade shows the remodeled roof and its new form.

2 The house front preserves the distinguishing markers of the building in a contemporary way.

3 First floor plan

4 Ground floor plan

5 Section

Can Tomeu

Sant Pere de Ribes, Spain

The restoration of this historic masterpiece was done with utmost respect to its original structure.

20

Located at the entrance of the Parc Natural de Garraf, Can Tomeu is one of the buildings belonging to the Masia Corral d'en Capdet, which was built around the year 1800 for agricultural an stone-crafting purposes. It is a piece of Catalan history and a national monument, meaning that the infrastructure needs to be kept in its original state wherever possible.

Can Tomeu was originally intended for the labour force of the larger masia, which was responsible for the maintenance of the entire finca. With time the abandoned building slowly deteriorated into a ruin, leaving only its bearing walls. The main purpose of the project was to restore the historical Catalan building to its original state while using the opportunity to increase the volume by 30 percent by creating an annex. Focusing on the original structure as the main volume and entrance juxtaposes the more modest yet modern extension. This keeps the building in line with its history while redesigning the interior to create a new spatial experience with clear and strong geometrical lines.

The construction of each of the sections was approached differently. The existing walls were reinforced with concrete on the inside, allowing them to return to their full original height while showcasing the old façade on the outside. The new annex in contrast is built in modern style. The entrance was moved to the old wine cellar, leading into the central room of the house with its astonishing double height. Central room and annex with kitchen and living room offer a full view into the park and the Mediterranean countryside. Two bedrooms are located to the left of the central room, each with its own ensuite bathroom; another bedroom can be found on the second floor. The outside space between the annex and a longitudinal pond allows to fully experience the vast expanse of the park.

1

2

1 The old walls are preserved by adding concrete only where needed.

2 The new annex adds a modern and futuristic twist to the old masia.

1

2

3

20

ARCHITECT
Andrea Solé Arquitectes

COMPLETION
2018

ORIGINAL BUILDING
1800

GROSS FLOOR AREA BEFORE | AFTER
70 m² | 120 m²

NUMBER OF ROOMS BEFORE | AFTER
1 | 3

4

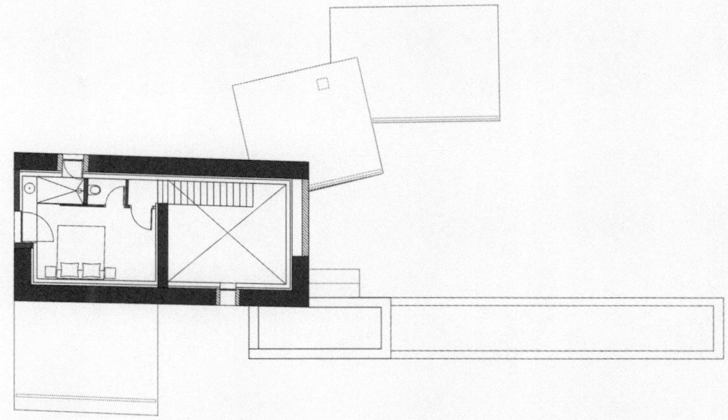

5

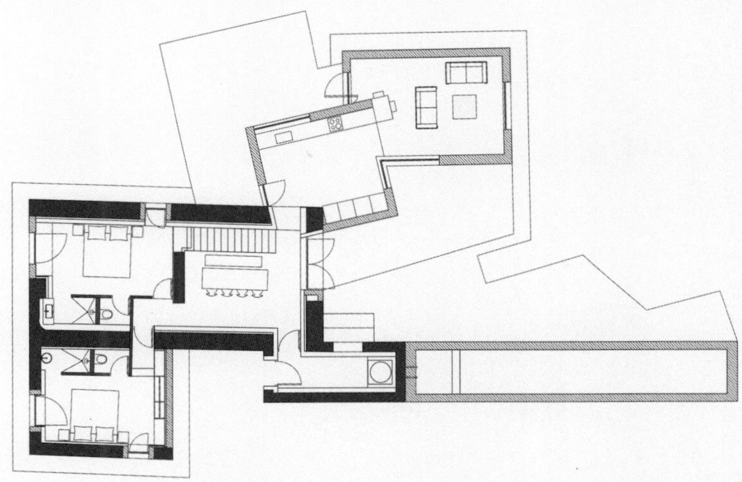

1 Big glass doors expand the space in the kitchen and the living room.

2 The texture of the original walls adds flair to the plain room.

3 Guests can enjoy a full view of the Garraf National Parc.

4 First floor plan

5 Ground floor plan

Cornish Cottage

Newquay, UK

This renovation retains the historical palimpsest of the walls with the new stone façade being a part of the house's ongoing history.

21

Located in the shadow of Saint Michael's Mount, this 400-year-old fisherman's cottage falls within the rare and ancient Dartmoor Longhouse vernacular. Jonathan Tuckey Design were charged with the task of renovating and creating an addition to the original structure, while protecting and enhancing this endangered typology. Reflecting on the design process, dealing with the building's long linear form, its compartmented sequence of numerous smaller rooms and absolutely irregular forms was a profoundly challenging task. Designed for a family who enjoys the outdoors, the house was conceived as a set of clearer defined spaces that act as routes through the property connecting the land to the sea.

A core design principle was the connection of the material palette to the local surroundings. The new addition was developed in this spirit, with the white lime of the main building substituted for a coarser stonework drawn directly from the next village. An internal passageway was formed of stone-lined walls and slate floor tiles, creating a sense of permanence and minerality. The new dry-stone-wall extension reaches out of the house, creating a guest bedroom on the upper level and an outside shower on its underside. The house is also linked to the ancient boat building techniques of the local area. These were displayed through the carefully and visibly human crafted details throughout the building, which were also a necessity, as no two material junctions were the same due to the irregular shapes of the rooms. Older walls have been insulated and restored, contrasting the newer walls, which are reminiscent of boat sails. The contrast between old and new is most apparent at the entrance to the study, which featured a framed doorway, with the existing curved wall creating two stacked openings. It perfectly shows the property's tailoring of new architecture to rest mutually with the existing.

1 The new dry-stone wall extension, which cantilevers out of the house, focuses on stone as a textural device.

1

1

2

3

4

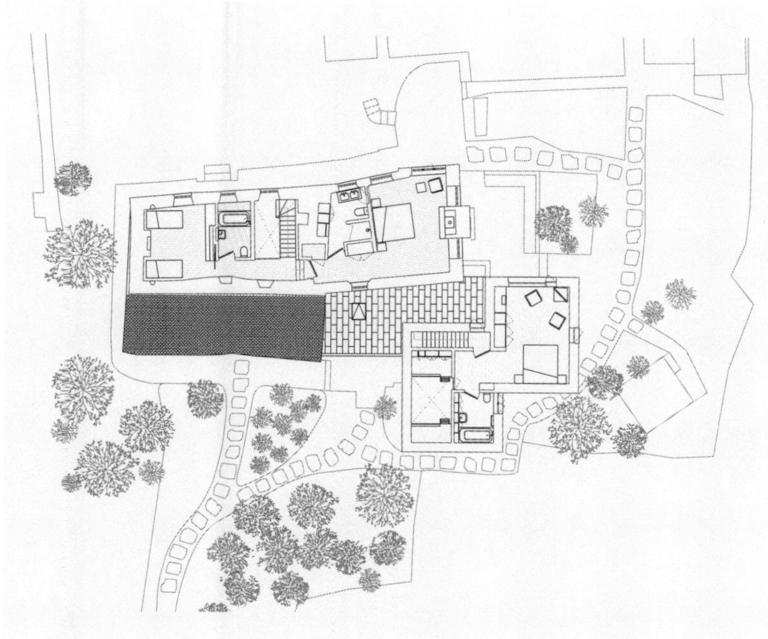

5

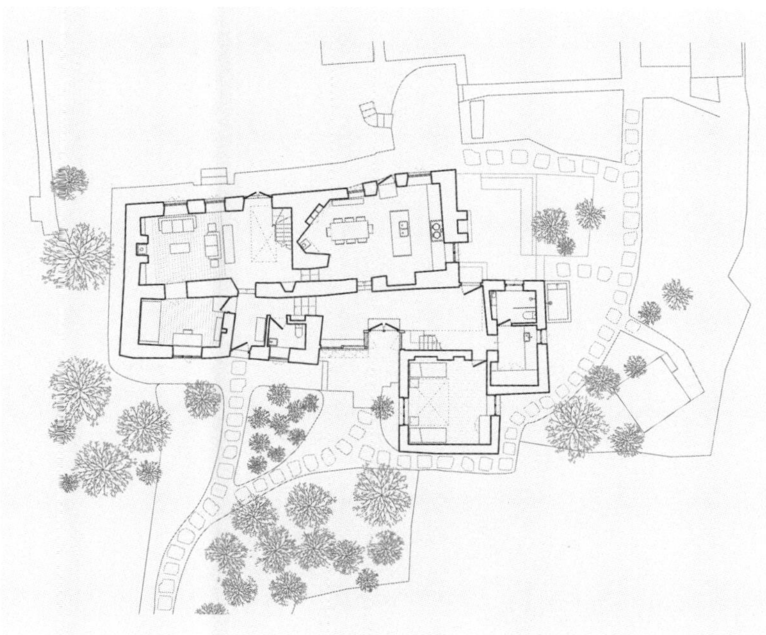

21

ARCHITECT
Jonathan Tuckey Design

COMPLETION
2019

ORIGINAL BUILDING
16th century

GROSS FLOOR AREA BEFORE | AFTER
220 m² | 250 m²

NUMBER OF ROOMS BEFORE | AFTER
13 | 16

1 Natural textures in walls and flooring evoke images of the farm cottage this building once was.

2 Retention and re-adaptation were two primary objectives while renovating the original cottage.

3 The old softly curved entrance is juxtaposed by the clear and angular new entrance to the study.

4 First floor plan

5 Ground floor plan

Blanket of Steel

Vilvoorde, Belgium

A working-class house destroyed by fire was converted into a passive, environment-conscious house with a community purpose.

22

The client opted for a thorough renovation, in accordance with passive house standards and using sustainable materials. The ground floor is opened up and set up as a multifunctional space, which in addition to private living areas can also be used for occasional socio-cultural encounters in the neighborhood. Curtains allow for the division of the space and creation of an entrance area. The existing low-quality rear extension is removed and replaced by a volume that forms one whole with the main volume.

A significant slope places the garden about 95 centimeters lower than the front garden. This height difference is incorporated into the house: The ground floor, part of the rear annex, is lowered by 70 centimeters, thus creating a stronger relationship with the garden while ensuring a higher spatiality in the house. The former cellar serves as a technical room and is hidden behind a hatch in the floor. A new wooden staircase to the second floor with adjacent void brings light into the heart of the house.

The front façade, sloping roof surfaces, and rear façade are clad with white metal sandwich panels, which create unity in the volume. Balancing the stimulating, surrounding urban fabric and integrating it into the context were core ideas realized in this project. The large window on the ground floor of the façade, and the view through to the back garden function as an inviting signal when the multifunctional space is used as a meeting place.

1 A recessed, wooden, and open staircase lets light deep into the house.

2 A glass front merges interior and exterior together.

3 The living room acts as a central meeting point.

1

2

22

ARCHITECT
Atelier Tom Vanhee

COMPLETION
2020

ORIGINAL BUILDING
1920

GROSS FLOOR AREA BEFORE | AFTER
140 m² | 143 m²

NUMBER OF ROOMS BEFORE | AFTER
3 | 3

ENGINEER OF STRUCTURE
Lime

3

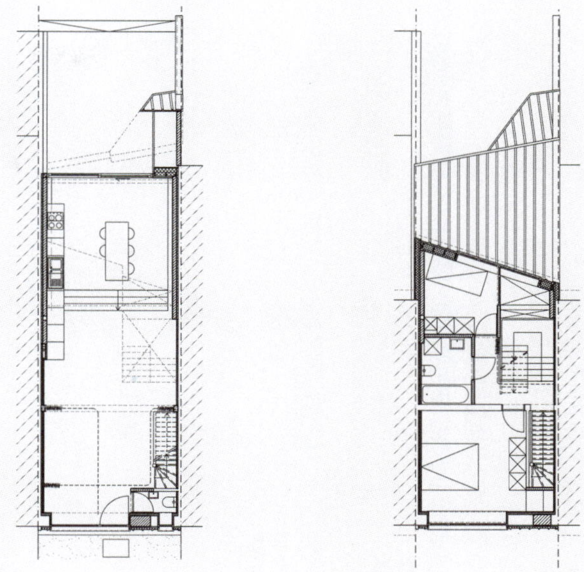

4

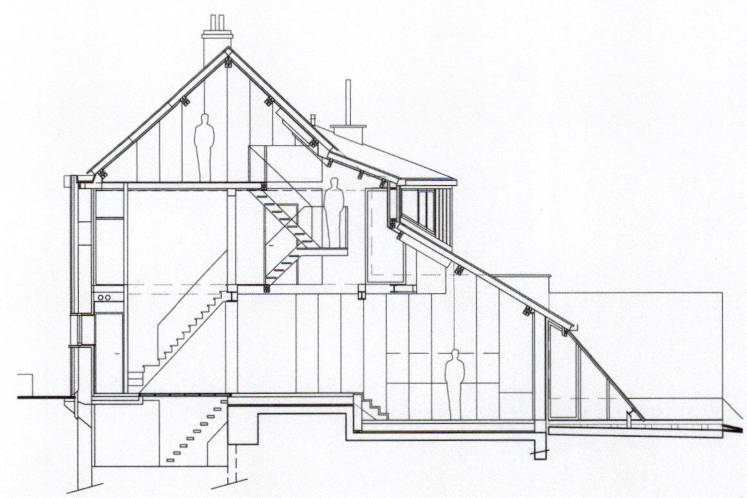

1 The construction of the house is open and light-flooded.

2 The remains of the old walls lend the bedroom a rustic look.

3 Ground and second floor plan

4 Section.

Lambeth Marsh House

London, UK

Warm light flows out of the house giving insights into the modern interior of the traditional shell.

23

BANHAM
LEE

Lambeth Marsh House was originally developed for artisan workers – in the form of modest, brick-built terraced houses, fronting conventional streets. The house had been left unoccupied for over ten years and is a two-story listed house situated within a conservation area in Lambeth, London.

The concept and challenge was to breathe new life into all floors while respecting the heritage of this listed building and restoring some of the lost historic detailing. Materiality was very important to help produce an appropriate contemporary design, assisting the architects' conservationist approach. The run-down fabric of the existing building required extensive refurbishment with particular sensitivity. Restoring the paneled fireplaces, wood paneling, architraves and skirting to their original condition celebrates the history of this building, while the addition of a contemporary rear and side extension compliment and update these features. Throughout the traditional setting, contemporary furniture within the spaces connect the old to the new, modern living. The ground floor has been opened up and transformed into a large open plan living space that creates a new light airy space with a glazed extension feeding light into every corner of the building.

1 The glass ceiling naturally illuminates the dining area and accentuates it in the shared kitchen space.

2 A beam framing the wall and ceiling spatially separates the rooms without inserting a wall.

1

2

1

2

3

4

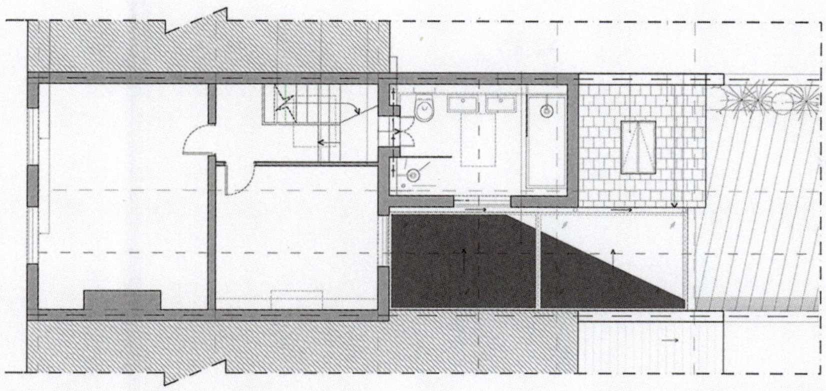

5

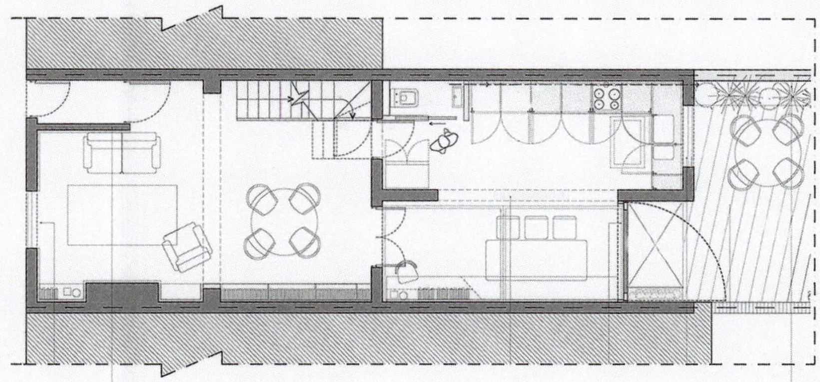

1 The minimalistic bedroom interior projects a modest and calm lifestyle.

2 The squared bookshelf melts into the pattern of the wooden wall panels.

3 Bathroom and bedroom are directly connected by an unobstructed passage.

4 First floor plan

5 Ground floor plan

23

ARCHITECT
Fraher & Findlay Architects

COMPLETION
2015

ORIGINAL BUILDING
1800s

GROSS FLOOR AREA BEFORE | AFTER
87 m² | 103 m²

NUMBER OF ROOMS BEFORE | AFTER
6 | 7

House CR

Caldas da Rainha, Portugal

The shape of the roof elevates the simple design of the house front.

24

The refurbishment of this house, built in the 1930s, was a very time sensitive manner for the architects. Located in Caldas de Rainha, it is culturally significant as part of the urban area that emerged at the beginning of the 20th century, west of the railway line that divided the entire city. Over the years all the remakes and remodels imposed on the structure have naturally worn off and started disintegrating. The house was in an advanced state of decay, with the existing damage only accelerating its deterioration if no action was taken. The aim of the project was simply to restore the original purpose as a private dwelling.

Kitchen and dining are directly accessible from the front of the house, while the living room retreats itself to the back. Three floor length windows provide a focused view of the courtyard. Before the intervention the garden had served all kinds of purposes from chicken coop to outbuilding. Now beautifully restored, the patio, surrounded by four-meter-high walls, offers a rare sense of intimacy, contrasting the bustling noise of the city.

A servicing nucleus, containing the designer stair case and bathroom, is placed in the center of the house, with another bathroom upstairs. It simultaneously serves as a room divider, naturally separating the dining and living area on the ground floor, and the two bedrooms on the first floor. The use of a neutral color palette and natural textures such as marble, wood, and ceramic keep the interior of the rooms minimalistic.

1

1 Soft fabric balances out the heavy stone kitchen counter.

1

2

3

24

ARCHITECT
Gonçalo Duarte Pacheco Arquitectos

COMPLETION
2017

ORIGINAL BUILDING
1936

GROSS FLOOR AREA BEFORE | AFTER
120 m² | 120 m²

NUMBER OF ROOMS BEFORE | AFTER
4 | 4

4

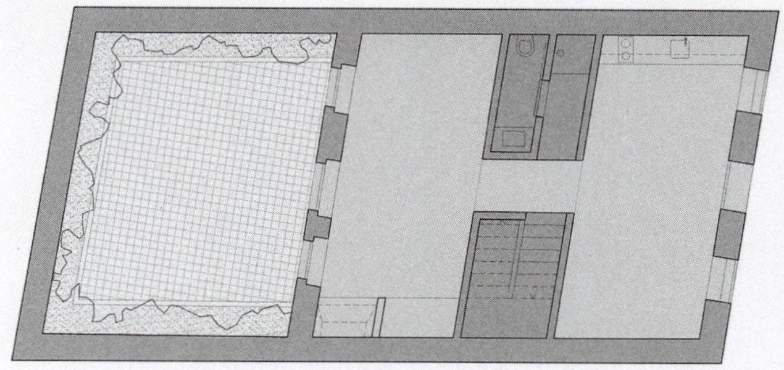

5

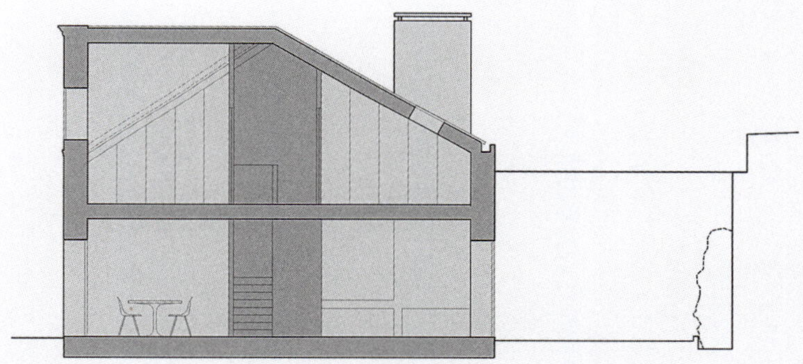

1 The floor length windows function as entries to the courtyard.

2 The staircase in the nucleus symbolically lifts itself of the ground.

3 The gray and white color scheme blends with the marble sink.

4 Ground floor plan

5 Section

Shmerling 8

Tel Aviv, Israel

The façade of the house was remodeled after paintings.

25

Originally built in Tel-Aviv's oldest neighborhood, Neve Tzedek, this project on Shmerling Street pairs its 19th-century origins with timelessly modern twists. As a building listed within the Tel Aviv municipality preservation plan, it was necessary to rejuvenate it to its original state. Succumbing to decades of neglect and dereliction, the residence presented the architects with various challenges. Most noteworthy, the original façade was partially destroyed and void of any architectural documentation to aid in its restoration. What resulted was a piecemeal process of assembling various historical documents, including an original painting by the famous Israeli painter Nachum Gutman, to realize restoration.

Additional aspects of the preservation process consisted of exposing and reinforcing an original wall made of native Kurkar stone, restoring welding details, and installing new wooden windows. The original plaster hue was recreated according to old paintings of the house and its surroundings. The strict guidelines that came with preserving the façade meant that the interior layout had to be adjusted around it. The works done on the façade resulted in an irregular lineup of the apartments and balconies, as well as uneven floor levels within the five living units. Steps and built-in benches were introduced between the exterior balconies and the interior living spaces.

The interior of the units was transformed with modern attributes and a natural color palette. Painted cement tiles were paired with bright wooden flooring. A gray kitchen with stainless steel counter tops was juxtaposed with handmade furniture made by local design studio Nachshon.

1 Simple furniture keeps the room uncluttered and spacious.

1

1

2

3

25

ARCHITECT
Muhlbauer Architects

COMPLETION
2018

ORIGINAL BUILDING
19th century

GROSS FLOOR AREA BEFORE | AFTER
280 m² | 380 m²

NUMBER OF ROOMS BEFORE | AFTER
19 | 22

3

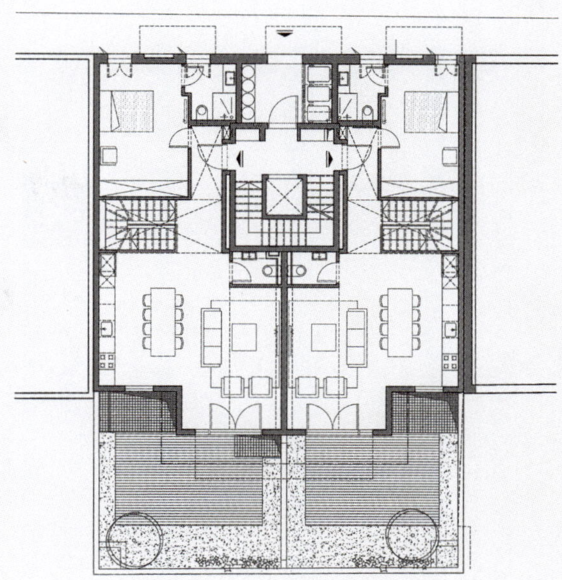

4

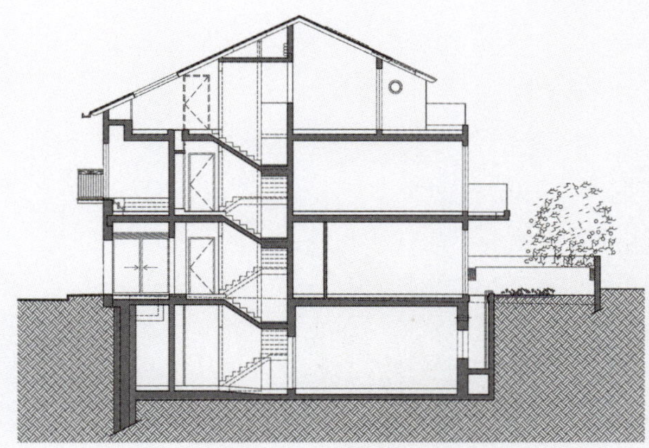

1 The balcony can be accessed directly from the living room.

2 The neutral colored door subtly accents the bright pink façade.

3 The simplistic shutter provides privacy for all windows, especially the ones on street level.

4 Ground floor plan

5 Section

Fitzroy House

Fitzroy, Australia

A compact terrace house was turned into a functioning family house.

26

This renovation and extension to a narrow single-fronted terrace house was the beginning of a family's unconventional move from suburbia to inner city Fitzroy. The clients sought to create an edgy yet comfortable urban home for themselves and their two grown-up children.

The challenge was to transform a compact terrace house into a functioning family home. As the heritage fabric of the building had been heavily modified over the years, Mitsuori Architects had the unique opportunity to entirely redefine the spaces within the building. A light-filled communal living room forms the heart of the home, with a sculpted plywood ceiling above a two-story void that brings an abundance of natural light into the space. Existing brickwork was salvaged and re-used for the new portions of the house, with reverse brick veneer providing a beautiful visual feature internally, as well as a thermally efficient wall construction to the new living space. Recycled timber beams were incorporated into the structure of the building in response to the client's love of timber and connection to the timber industry.

The home's private spaces are tucked into other parts of the house, making use of all available space and creating a sense of separation and privacy. On the upper floor, two separate bedroom zones are connected via a staircase and an open walkway linking across to a rooftop balcony. The lower level utilizes skylights to draw light deep into the house, creating a serene ambiance to the master bathroom and providing a dramatic view of the sky from the bath.

This project demonstrates that a small footprint is no barrier to creating a functional family home that is both unexpected and deceptively spacious.

1 The exposed brickwall and dark colors lend the living room an industrial yet modern look.

1

1

2

3

4

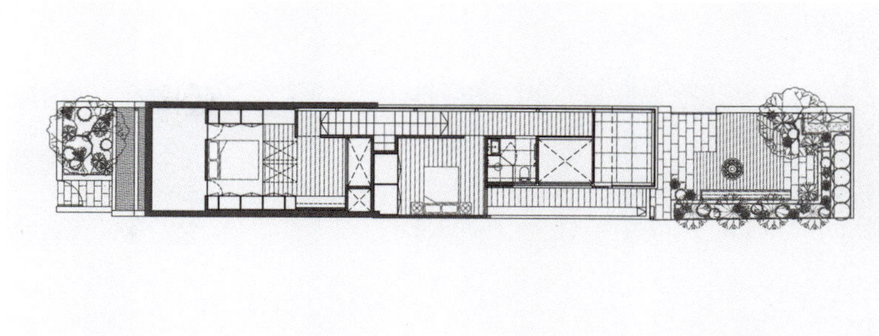

5

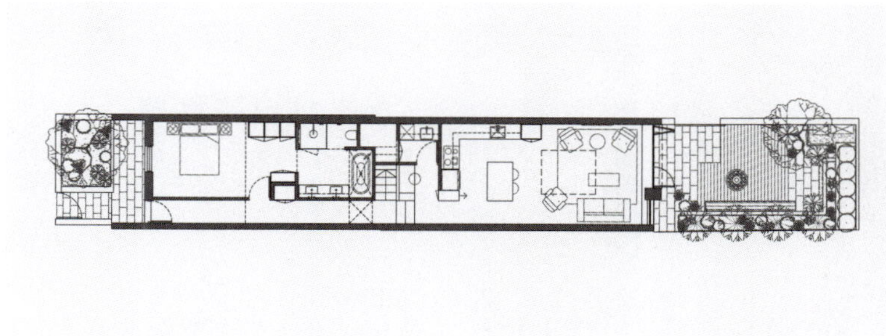

26

ARCHITECT
Mitsuori Architects

LANDSCAPE ARCHITECT
Andrew Plant Landscapes

COMPLETION
2020

ORIGINAL BUILDING
1890s

GROSS FLOOR AREA BEFORE | AFTER
115 m^2 | 160 m^2

NUMBER OF ROOMS BEFORE | AFTER
5 | 7

1 The terrace offers a comfortable and private seating area.

2 Timber wood beams are shown through in the kitchen ceiling.

3 The kitchen is characterized by dark surfaces.

4 First floor plan

5 Ground floor plan

Fritz Frees Himself

Landshut, Germany

The historic photos show the original state in 1948 and the modifications in 1957 and 1975. The renovation restored the clear forms.

27

The house is centrally located in Landshut in the immediate vicinity of Trausnitz Castle. The single-family house was built in 1948. In 1955 a first extension took place and in 1975 it was finally remodeled. The substance of the construction stages falls sharply in quality, in terms of material and value. The original residential building from 1948 is worth preserving, especially because the floor plan typology is characterized by great flexibility and timeless functionality. The renovation design is based on the aesthetics and proportions of the first construction phase. On the east and north sides reminiscences of the annexes are retained but are clearly distinguished from the main building in their materialization.

The ground floor remains largely unchanged in terms of space and organization. On the upper floor the bedrooms each have access via a ladder staircase to a gallery in the attic. The ceilings are generously opened upwards. The roof truss was renewed for spatial as well as energetic reasons. The façade and windows are upgraded for energy efficiency. In terms of construction technology, the area of the east façade with a dormer picks up on the research project "TES Energy Façade" of the Chair of Design and Timber Construction at the Technical University of Munich. Here, a prefabricated wooden stud wall with pre-installed insulation and windows is placed in front of the existing building, which, in addition to its insulating function, also takes over the static load transfer of dormer and roof. Thanks to the very high degree of prefabrication, the construction time for the roof and façade renovation was reduced to just two weeks.

Another essential design theme is the barrier-free and thus also sustainable use of the house in old age. The first floor was therefore designed as an independently functioning, barrier-free living unit with a bedroom and wheelchair-accessible shower room.

1 The fireplace separates the living area and the dining area.

2 Light colors dominate the kitchen.

1

2

1

2

27

ARCHITECT
DWA David Wolfertstetter Architektur

COMPLETION
2020

ORIGINAL BUILDING
1948

GROSS FLOOR AREA BEFORE | AFTER
515 m² | 335 m²

NUMBER OF ROOMS BEFORE | AFTER
18 | 12

3

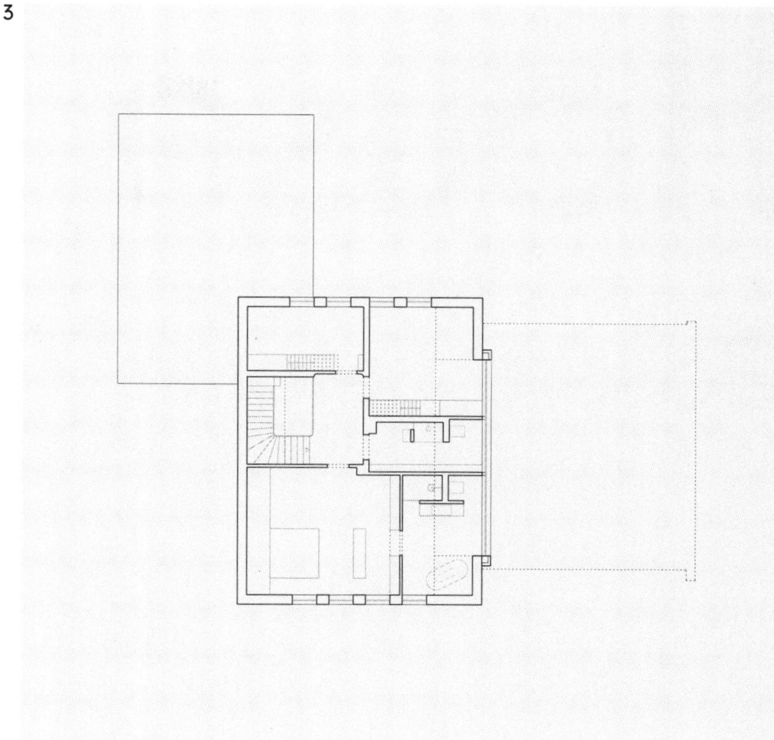

4

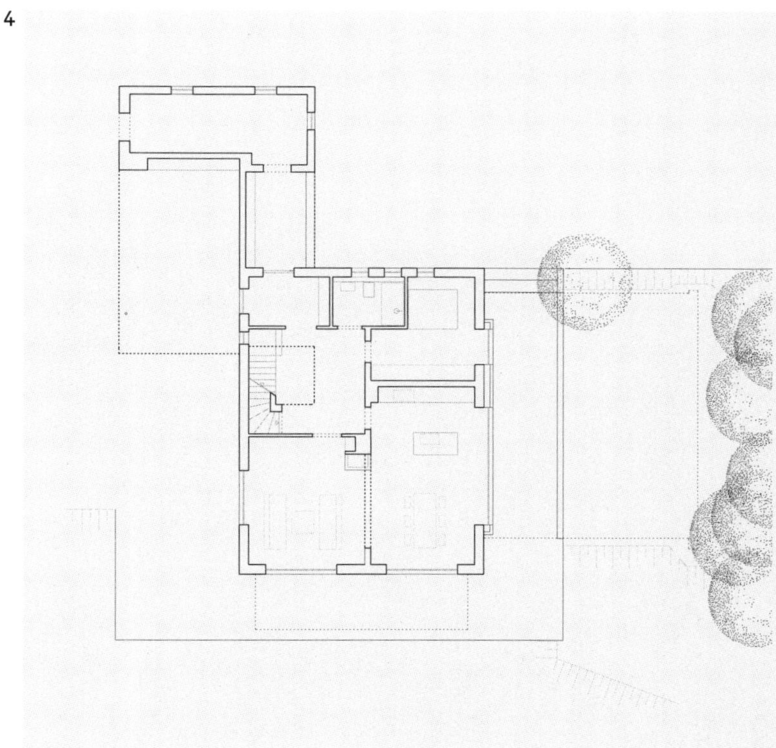

1 The renovated staircase retains its original charm.

2 Smart storage solutions can be found in the children's room.

3 First floor plan

4 Ground floor plan

House BS

Gavere, Belgium

The historic family farm is visibly revitalized by the mix of white and red brick house wing textures surrounding the central patio.

28

The farm is located in a valley at the intersection of small meandering streets with terraced houses to the east, vast old orchards to the west, and the alluvial plain of the Scheldt to the south. This cluster, included in the architectural heritage inventory, consists of the dwelling, stables, and the bread house, with a central square overlooking the façades of the terraced houses. The brick volumes and their gable roofs, the use of materials, form, and typology are very specific to the area, yet vary in size and layout in a very fascinating way.

The expansion is based on this diversity, providing two additional volumes with gable roofs. Interventions within the existing volumes were done only where strictly necessary, especially for circulation purposes. Two symmetrical wings were added on the west side of the main volume, creating a patio with an enclosed character. By not connecting the two volumes, a simple passage to the garden was created, allowing the volumes to remain visually separate from each other, which reinforces the cluster idea.

1

2

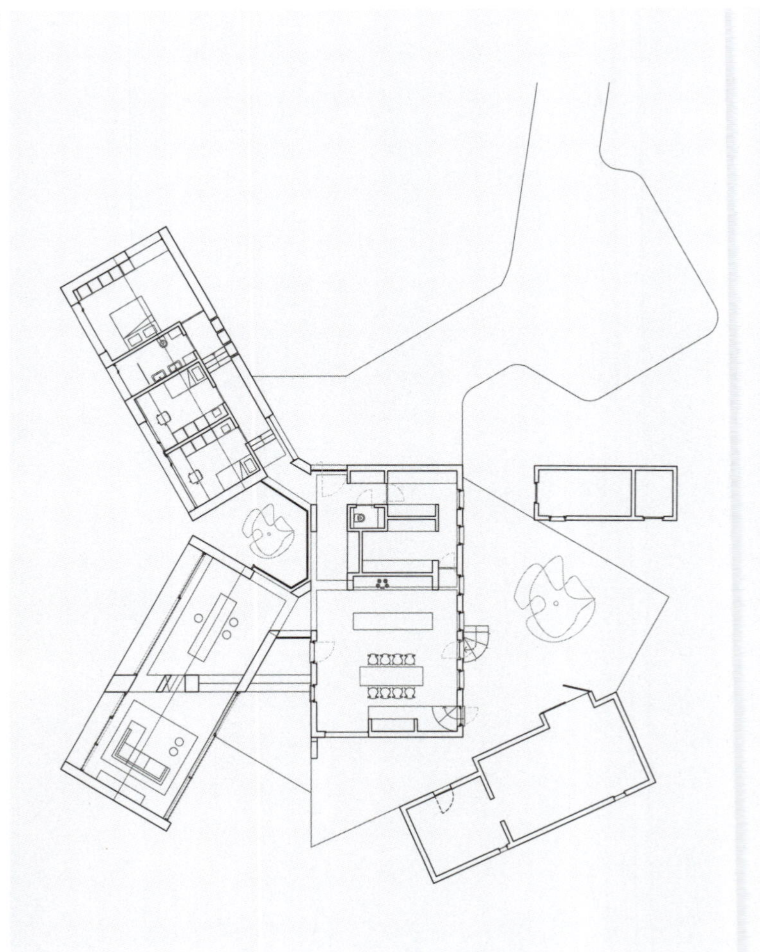

3

1 The new fireplace serves as a room divider in the contemporary interior.

2 Ground floor plan

3 The wooden beams remain the focal point in the kitchen and dining area.

28

ARCHITECT
Graux & Baeyens architecten

LANDSCAPE ARCHITECT
burO Groen

COMPLETION
2017

ORIGINAL BUILDING
1850-1900

GROSS FLOOR AREA BEFORE | AFTER
195 m² | 320 m²

NUMBER OF ROOMS BEFORE | AFTER
6 | 12

Croft Lodge Studio

Herrefordshire, UK

The ruin, held together by ivy, was preserved parallel to the creation of a new house and studio.

29

The architects were asked to conserve this curtilage, listed overgrown ruin by the local conservation office. Immediately it raised the question of which parts of this historic structure were worth conserving and how to do it affordably. Their strategy provided the answer to both these questions.

They encapsulated the 300-year-old ruin within a new building that provided both thermal comfort and structural support. A steel portal frame was erected over the ruin, which was then infilled with timber, sheeted with OSB board, insulated, wrapped in a waterproof membrane and finally clad in black corrugated iron. This was the cheapest solution, as the architects carried out much of the work in their spare time, and it also resulted in minimum intervention to the ruin itself. The new envelope closely follows the form of the original building, making parts of the building, which have collapsed over time, legible again. These are the ghost spaces, formed from contemporary materials – plain, precise, and minimal – all readily available from the local industrial estate.

Everything is preserved: The original timber frame with the carpenters' marks, peeling lime plaster, birds nests and dead bats, abandoned fixtures and even the dead ivy. There is no hierarchy of value but instead a story of occupation. The different lives of this building can be seen in what has been preserved and what has been added. It allows for both continuity and change – a dynamic contemporary space within the form of a building that has stood on the same site for over three centuries.

1 The studio space showcases the enclosed ruin without intruding on it.

1

1

2

3

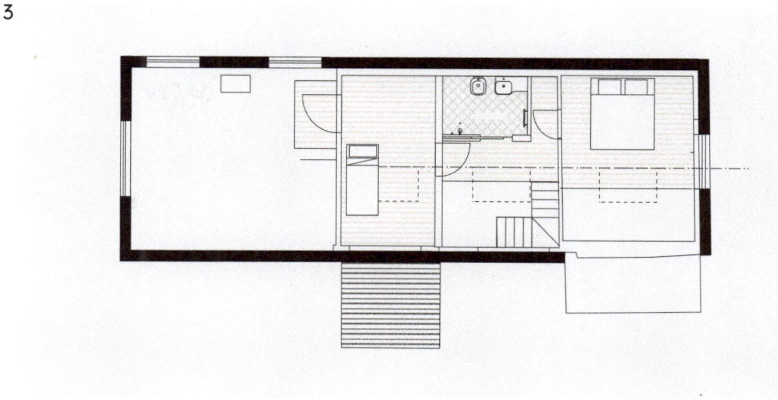

4

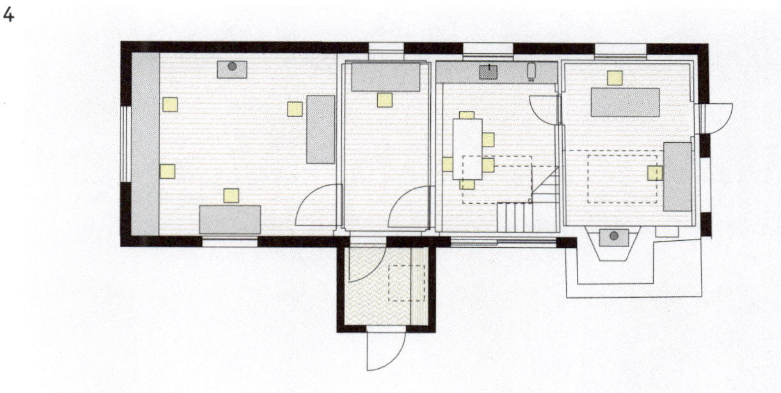

1 The living room features the original fireplace and bread oven.

2 The kitchen units are free standing in order not to touch the ancient walls.

3 First floor plan

4 Ground floor plan

29

ARCHITECT
Kate Darby Architects
David Connor Design

COMPLETION
2017

ORIGINAL BUILDING
18th century

GROSS FLOOR AREA BEFORE | AFTER
100 m² | 150 m²

NUMBER OF ROOMS BEFORE | AFTER
6 | 7

Mar Mediterráneo 34

Mexico City, Mexico

The original façade has been restored without changing its iconic design.

30

Tacuba is one of Mexico City's neighborhoods located northwest of downtown. It is full of cultural and architectural heritage and has undergone social and urban transformations that have lasted to this day. Many vestiges forged at different times can be found here. Among these the Mar Mediterráneo 34, built in 1910, remained, surrounded by abandoned or collapsed buildings. It is thus historically significant to the National Institute of Fine Arts and the National Institute of Anthropology and History. The goal of the intervention was to create a legacy that encourages the transformation of Tacuba, enhancing and rescuing its heritage, by taking advantage of existing spaces in a sustainable way to give life to this magical neighborhood.

To achieve that, original elements of the façade were restored with replacement pieces made by local artisans. This recovers the main elements such as the carved quarry, the iron railings, the large windows and the glass roof tiles. The historic layout of the courtyard features a set of original lattice portals opposite the floors raised to double height, which focuses the gaze on the sky in a play of light and shadow. The entrance baseboard made of volcanic stone surrounds the entire ground floor – a metaphorical foundation to lift the resurfaced history. The restored house has three levels and seven apartments, which interact with the main patio through two additional terraces. New interior spaces are flexible and adapt to contemporary lifestyle, creating an interconnected home that distinguishes itself through its simplicity. Intermediate floors by Efrain Hernández, who also did the construction, were installed to make optimal use of the double height rooms. To go beyond the selection of materials for sustainability, the integration of vegetation avoids an increase of the urban footprint. All those carefully taken measures turn this project into a new layer of the city, preserving the marks left by the flow of time.

1

1 A mezzanine ensures efficient use of the extra space in the new double height rooms.

1

2

3

30

ARCHITECT
Inca Hernández

INTERIOR DESIGN:
Ana Ximena García,
Gabriela Llovera, Raíz Mx,
Adrián González

COMPLETION
2020

ORIGINAL BUILDING
1910

GROSS FLOOR AREA BEFORE | AFTER
270 m² | 620 m²

NUMBER OF ROOMS BEFORE | AFTER
3 | 10

4

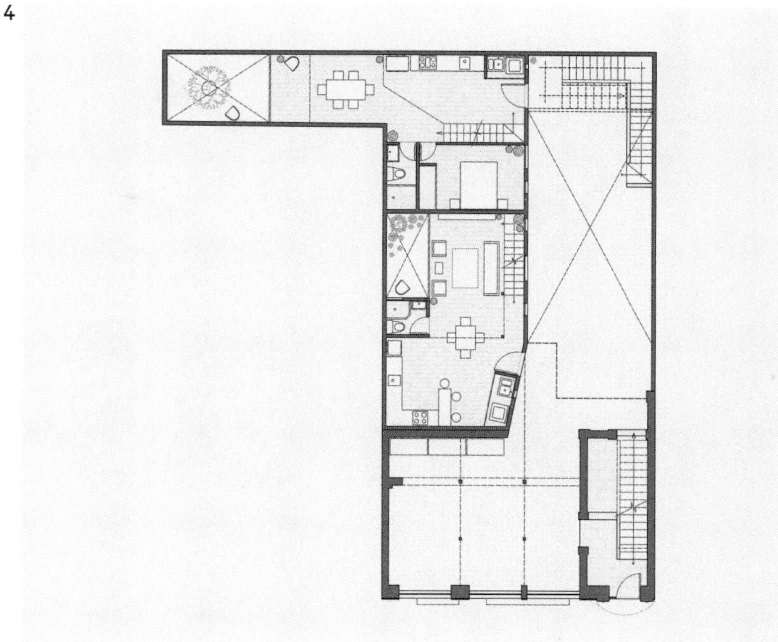

5

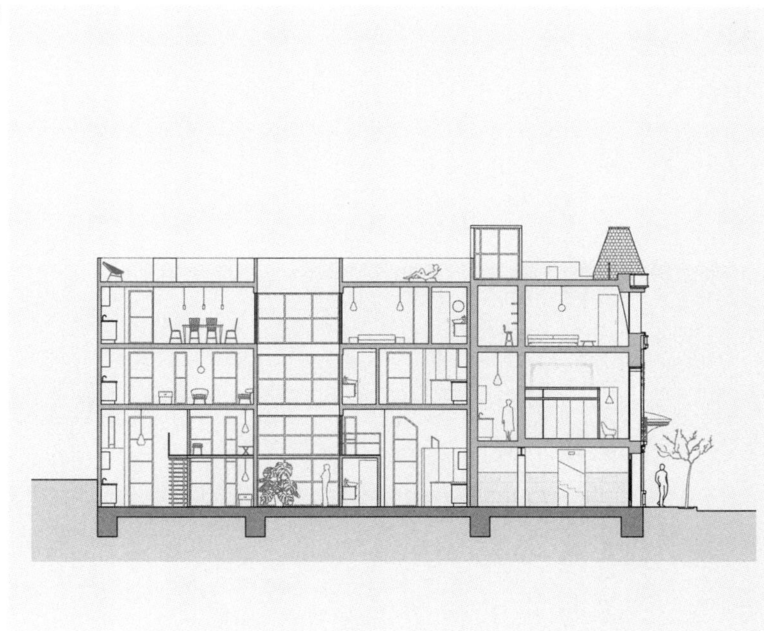

1 The lattice arrangement is a simple but creative privacy screen.

2 Shining in through the courtyard, intricate light patterns freckle the walls of the bedroom.

3 The charming interior is decorated using antique furniture pieces.

4 Ground floor plan

5 Section

House in Kawasaki

Ise, Japan

The iconic wooden house fronts and the gabled roof structures have been maintained since the Edo period.

31

This project is located in an area of Kawasaki's Mie Prefecture where the townscape of the Edo period still remains. The main house of a well-known, long-established general merchandise wholesaler in Ise, originally built in 1929, needed to be repaired and renovated. Today, this house is a family home and thus needed adaptations to current lifestyle and interior design suited for raising children. However, the gabled roof and the exterior of the building are symbolic structures of the area, so it was necessary to keep the shape of the building as unchanged as possible.

The dining room, kitchen, bedrooms, and bathrooms are arranged to place the Tatami room and the guest room between them. These had not been used for a long time. Wanting to preserve them, the plastering and other work that had inadvertently caused severe damage in the past were returned to their original state. Shoji screens, room dividers made of translucent sheets on a lattice frame, are used to gently connect the rooms in the buildin
This allows the movement of peo-
ple within the house to flow evenl
and free of congestion.

The architects pass this building
to many future generations by in-
corporating contemporary lifesty
into the design, while also payin
respect to the history and longev
of the building and the townscap
surrounding it. To achieve that, tr
ditional construction methods an
materials were used in the design
finishing of each space. The textu
of these materials will change wit
the passing of time, gradually
blending the old and the new int
each other.

1 The Japanese style Tatami room features an open view into the garden.

2 Wooden interior design can be found in the entire house.

3 Translucent Shoji screens allow for natural light to enter the room.

1

2

3

1

2

3

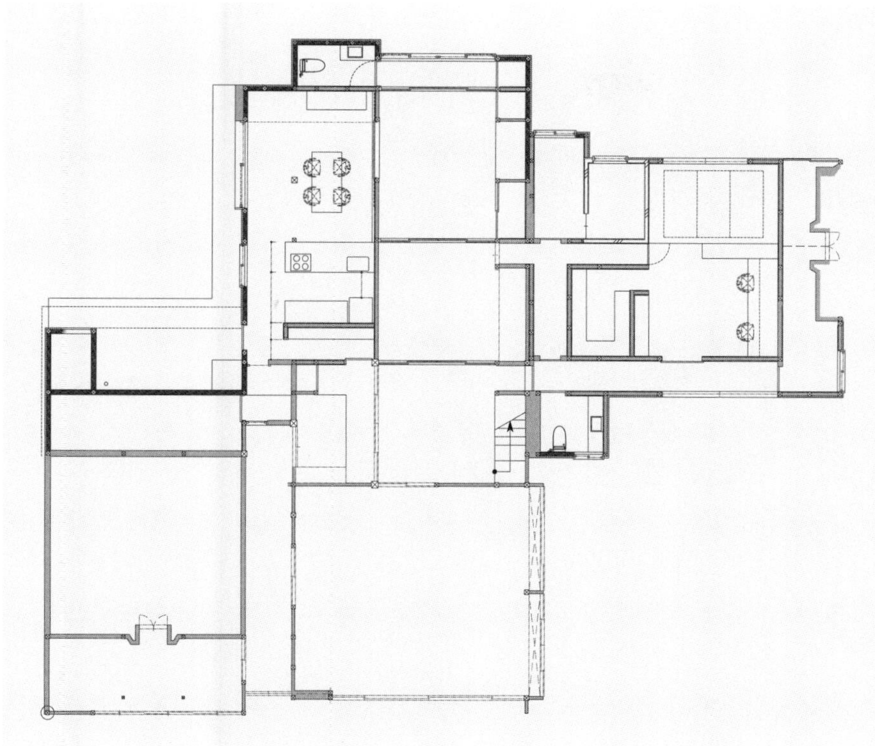

31

ARCHITECT
Koyori

INTERIOR DESIGN
Koyori
with
Atelier Salt

COMPLETION
2020

ORIGINAL BUILDING
1929

GROSS FLOOR AREA BEFORE | AFTER
330 m² | 330 m²

NUMBER OF ROOMS BEFORE | AFTER
11 | 7

1 The kitchen design matches the wooden aesthetic of the house.

2 Natural colors project a calm and minimalistic atmosphere.

3 Ground floor plan

Sand Dune Sanctuary

Sorrento, Australia

The relaxed family home evokes memories of the beach shack it once was.

32

A mid-century beach shack occupied this site on an unmade tea tree lined road near the Back Beach on the Mornington Peninsula. The architects wanted to retain the essence of the relaxed holiday house experience, whilst providing a classic, long-lasting, high-quality house that knows its place. References include the modernity and detailing of Ludwig Mies van der Rohe and Richard Neutra to situate the project in a context of international and cross-century design awareness.

A ramp accesses the first floor living quarters, while the ground floor is tailored specifically for guests. Underfloor space was reclaimed to create a man cave and car storage. True to the modernist ethos, space arrangement of the family and kitchen is social and outward looking. The open-plan living and custom interior design pay respect to successful and appropriate techniques of modernity. Windows are curated to focus the gaze on the surrounding tea tree tops while minimizing awareness of neighboring houses. Curtains and sliding screens give control over privacy, light and views. Solar cells cover the roof and wiring is provided for future batteries. Deep verandas, thermal mass, efficient lighting and appliances were incorporated.

The double story house is nestled into the natural sand dune landscape to keep a low profile from the street while providing sufficient floor area to meet the brief and maximizing the surrounding garden space. The natural, colored cladding and metals are sympathetic to the local Sorrento limestone and harmonize with the existing landscape. The clearing around the house protects it from bushfires while driveway surfaces are reinforced underneath the rolling grass.

The design of the house also focuses on flexibility for multi-generational living. The upper floor ramp alleviates worries about future access. The guest rooms can be transformed into living quarters, providing space for a second family.

1

2

1 The kitchen shows off the high-quality materials used in its construction.

2 The architecture, interior design and furniture were holistically integrated to create a harmonious result.

1

2

3

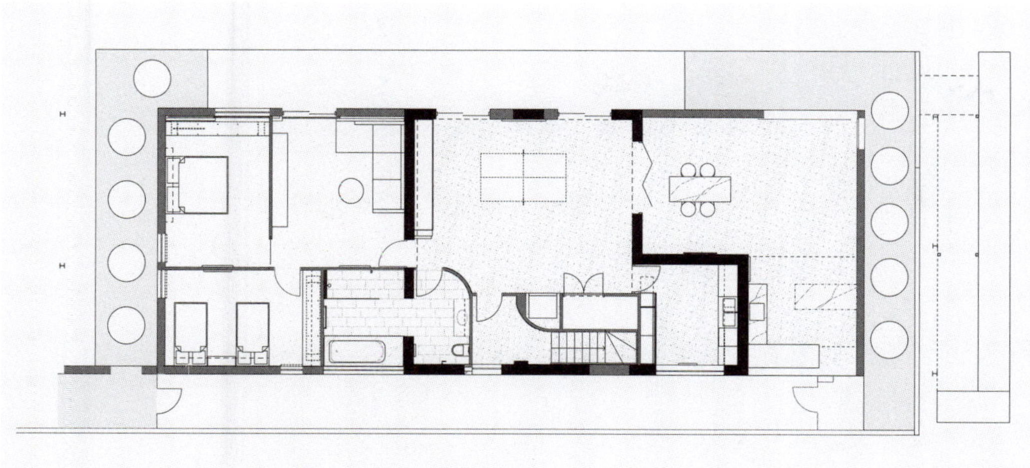

4

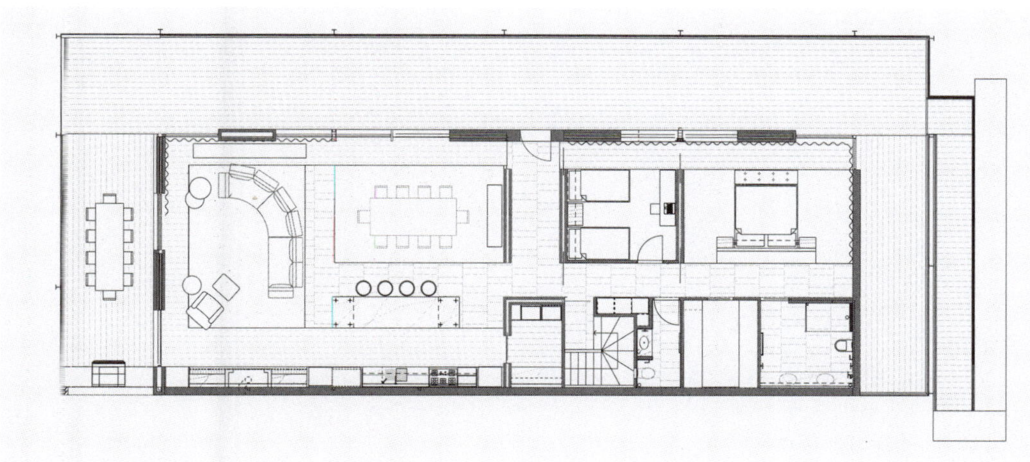

1 The beautiful, uncluttered, and highly functional spaces are free and feel uplifting.

2 Natural colors and textures transform the bathroom into a calm place of relaxation.

3 First floor plan

4 Ground floor plan

32

ARCHITECT
Hindley & Co

INTERIOR STYLING
Lees O'Rielly

COMPLETION
2019

ORIGINAL BUILDING
1960s

GROSS FLOOR AREA BEFORE | AFTER
215 m^2 | 240 m^2

NUMBER OF ROOMS BEFORE | AFTER
10 | 14

Rural House Restoration

Muros, Spain

The project idea seeks to highlight its identity: dignifying the preexisting and creating a fluid interior space bathed in light.

33

The house is located in Miraflores, Muros, a small rural core of traditional character, formed by a set of stone houses and granaries that once housed, dried, and treated the corn plantations. Situated on a steep plot, it was originally composed of two attached volumes, in line with the traditional Galician housing scheme that used stables and kitchen as the main spaces. However, over time a third volume was added, and a series of modifications were made that distorted its original character.

The three volumes were adapted to the slope, protected from winds and imposing views of the Muros estuary. This initially gave rise to a compartmentalized interior that was composed of small and dark spaces. The project proposal was based on the actual understanding of the place: The scale of the rural nucleus, the pre-existing housing, the materiality of the stone, the 180-degree views of the estuary, and the sunlight were parameters all taken into consideration during the planning. The original stone volumes were maintained with their historic form and façade, while the third added volume was replaced with a new volume of concrete with large windows that open onto the views of the estuary. Committing to a sincere use of materials limited the processing of the original stone and introduced exposed concrete and zinc to unify the roofs. Three skylights of different dimensions were created to flood everything from bathroom showers and dining room, to the old stables and interior stone walls with natural daylight.

The interior is considered as a fluid space which travels through different floors and rooms of the house and embraces the unique character of each area. Playing with the visual connections and the light gave the architects the possibility to create a continuous system that structures the spatial experience of the house.

1 Everywhere in the house light bathes the interior.

1

1

2

3

33

ARCHITECT
fuertespenedo arquitectos

COMPLETION
2018

ORIGINAL BUILDING
1911

GROSS FLOOR AREA BEFORE | AFTER
219 m² | 219 m²

NUMBER OF ROOMS BEFORE | AFTER
3 | 2

4

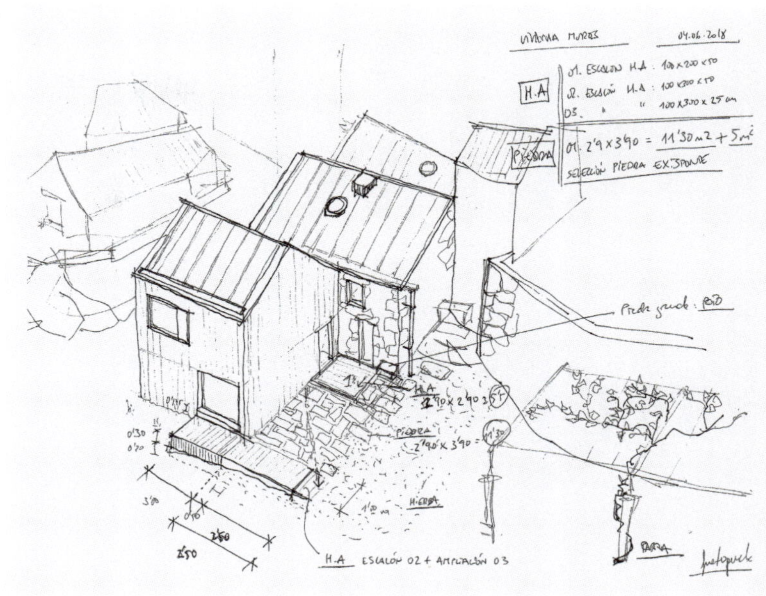

5

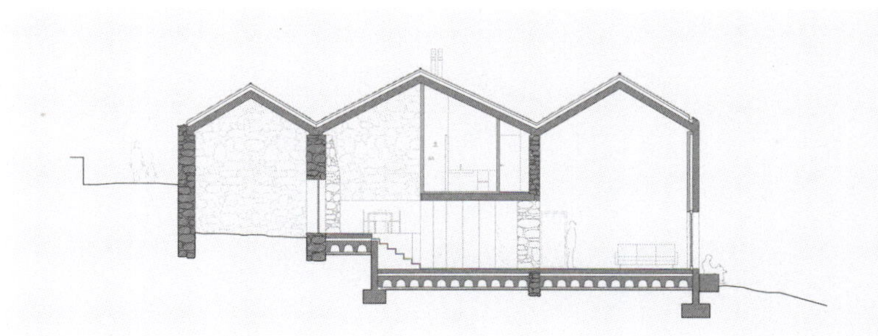

6

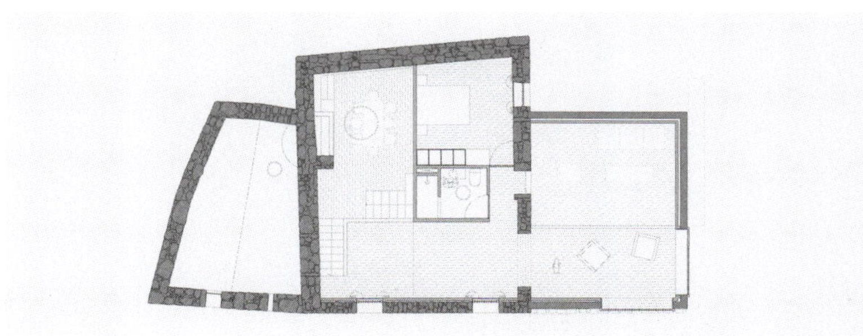

7

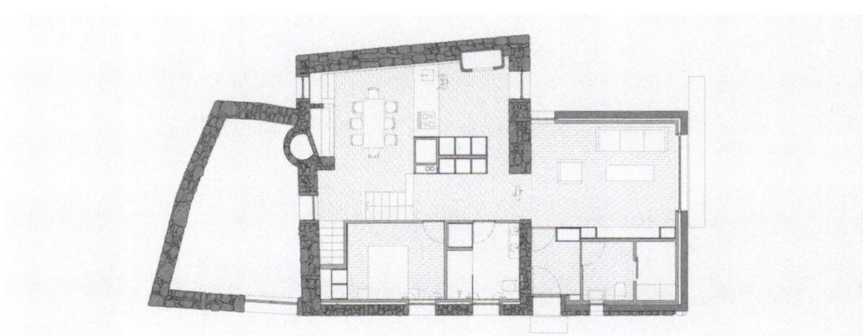

1 The original stone walls can be found throughout the interior.

2 The new concrete volume contains large windows that open onto the landscape.

3 The three volumes adapt to the environment in height, color and shape.

4 Sketch

5 Section

6 First floor plan

7 Ground floor plan

Berkley House

North Vancouver, Canada

The architect recognized the need to adapt the Californian style atmosphere to modern family needs.

34

The family of four was originally attracted to the Berkley House due to its front clerestory window, corner kitchen window, and post and beam configuration. By preserving these elements whilst modernizing the design, RSAAW transformed an older, inefficient house into an award-winning and thoroughly contemporary residence.

It was important to both the family and RSAAW to respect the original bones of the house and renovate as sustainably as possible. By donating the old millwork and appliances, repurposing the kitchen nook floor plate for the attic space, and upgrading all windows with triple glazing, RSAAW was able to keep the project economically and environmentally conscious.

Opening the floorplan circulation was an important unifying theme throughout the project. This was achieved by tearing down walls from the formerly galley-style kitchen, enlarging door openings, and removing and repurposing a basement mechanical room. The stairway floor was opened up to showcase the newly installed custom double-height atrium bookcase. Main floor ceilings were vaulted and punctured with large skylights. In addition to opening up the layout spatially, RSAAW upgraded and optimized thermal efficiencies to better suit the Canadian climate, completely replacing all insulation and installing in-floor heating.

Connecting the interior with North Vancouver's picturesque mountain backdrop, oversized glazing units placed throughout the home share views of temperate greenery and a backyard vegetable garden. The emphasis on light and space is expressed throughout the main floor, with threshold-free light oak flooring, shadow-line walls, and streamlined cabinetry adding depth and warmth. Further integrating with the surrounding environment, a custom garden treehouse is lightly wrapped around a Douglas fir with an engineered brace that allows the tree to grow without harm.

1 Previously a dining space on the main floor, pictured is the new double-height atrium with bookcase.

1

1

2

3

34

ARCHITECT
RSAAW

COMPLETION
2020

ORIGINAL BUILDING
mid-20th century

GROSS FLOOR AREA BEFORE | AFTER
260 m² | 260 m²

NUMBER OF ROOMS BEFORE | AFTER
4 | 4

4

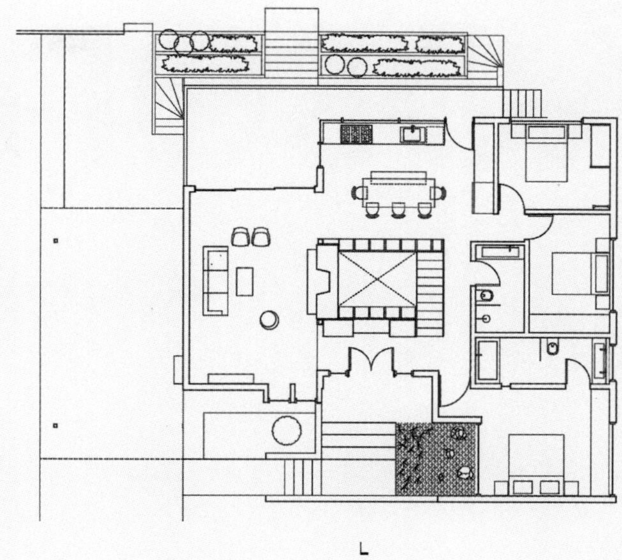

5

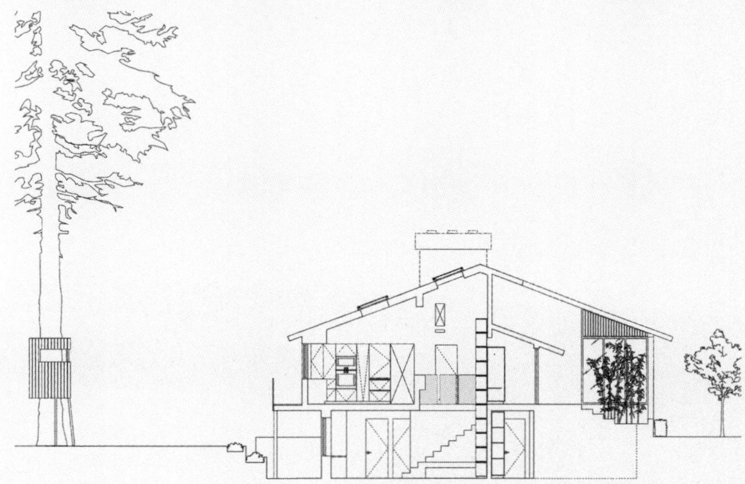

1 The corner window was dropped, triple glazed, and extended.

2 The dining area has transformed into a fully open space.

3 The ceiling in the parent's bedroom was also vaulted which makes it appear higher.

4 Upper floor plan

5 Section

Koser I

Iowa City, IA, USA

The form of the house lives on with the new modern aesthetic.

35

328

This 120 square meter home, built in 1960 and named "the shack" by neighbors, had a lot of potential. Close to a university such neglected, smaller homes are at high risk of becoming student rentals and, if the mix of owners and renters grows out of proportion, a flourishing neighborhood can disintegrate. With a gesture to prevent such an erosion while creating a right-sized family home, the house was completely renewed in layout, materiality, envelope, and supporting systems. The footprint was expanded to 232 square meter on the main level and the existing, smaller lower level was finished.

All windows were configured to accentuate the character of mid-century architecture and maximize daylight. A minimal palette of materials was consistently applied throughout and non-essential elements were removed. Doorjambs and wall base were held flush with the walls and all casing was eliminated. A high performance envelope was achieved using foamed-in-place insulation and insulated sheathing. New, highly efficient systems were installed, including a horizontally-bored geothermal system, a fresh air energy recovery system, and LED lighting. The photovoltaic roof array offsets any energy that is consumed. Success can be measured in the surplus of energy and credit received from the utility company since occupancy. It can also be measured in the positive influence made as other properties on the street have begun a similar renewal with the same goals – quality, sustainability, design excellence – all of which will further preserve the neighborhood.

1 The patio, accesible through the kitchen, offers an amazing view of the night sky.

1

1

2

35

ARCHITECT
Neumann Monson Architects

COMPLETION
2016

ORIGINAL BUILDING
1960

GROSS FLOOR AREA BEFORE | AFTER
120 m² | 232,25 m²

NUMBER OF ROOMS BEFORE | AFTER
7 | 13

3

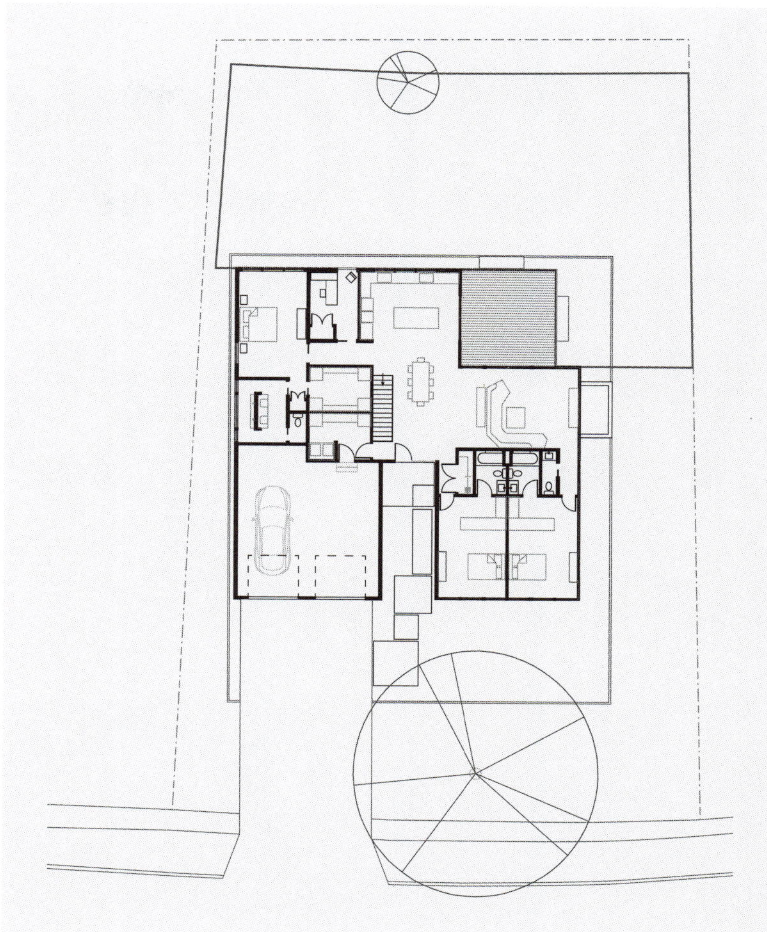

4

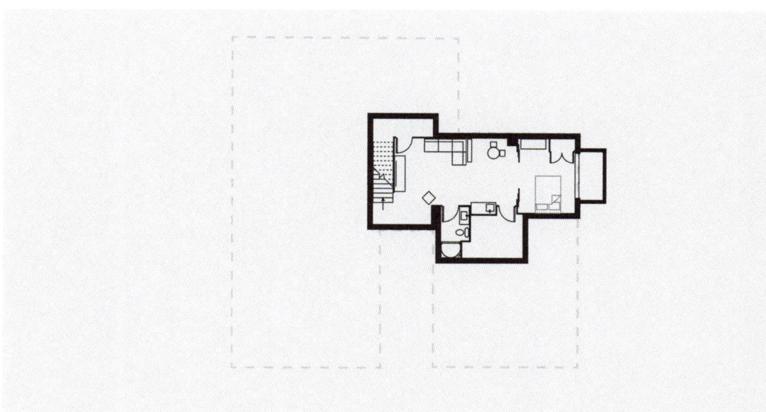

1 The spacious kitchen is modern and flooded with daylight.

2 The living room offers a calm and comfortable atmosphere.

3 Ground floor plan

4 Basement floor plan

Marqués de Vallejo 4
Logroño, Spain

The neighborhood is revitalized by the renovation of this early 20th century building.

36

HOTEL

This project involves the revitalization of a small abandoned part of the old town in the historic neighborhood of Ollerías Altas y Bajas, an urban area where the pottery industry of the city flourished during the Modern Age. Previously renovated in 1928 by architect Fernando Salvador Carreras, the building had been abandoned close to ruin for decades and was now rehabilitated for housing and commercial purposes.

All measures taken exclude demolition as an option in order to maintain the building's original alignment and to preserve the original layout of the urban fabric. This allowed the architects to convert the southern dividing wall into a real façade, taking advantage of the slight setback of the adjacent building. It also grants space for three new windows facing the beautiful Espolón square. The main challenge was to recover the bearing capacity of the original wooden structure. These bare structures are now integrated as a focal point in the interior design, which makes excellent use of their natural texture.

1

2

3

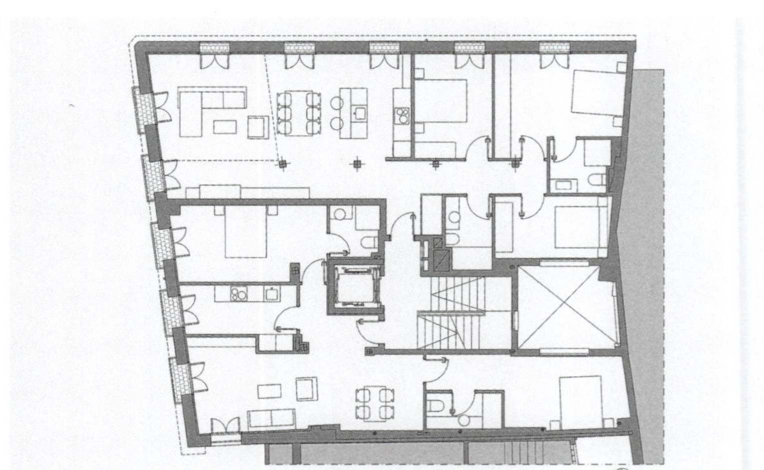

4

1 Even after the renovation, wooden structures shape the character of this building.

2 The minimalistic design choices exude an all-encompassing calmness.

3 Third floor plan

4 White walls and open windows flood the space with light.

36

ARCHITECT
Sergio Rojo estudio

COMPLETION
2018

ORIGINAL BUILDING
1928, Fernando Salvador Carreras

GROSS FLOOR AREA BEFORE | AFTER
1115.79 m² | 1115.79 m²

NUMBER OF ROOMS BEFORE | AFTER
34 | 27

House Grill-Reichenauer

Payerbach, Austria

The addition of the new volume respects the original building and creates a mutual atmospheric symbiosis.

37

The design of this conversion was based on a fundamental assumption: Architecture always has a temporary responsibility for a previously untouched piece of nature.

Construction is always an act of absorbing nature - thus at the beginning a garden is created, a hortus conclusus as the epitome of paradise. With every construction begins a time-limited responsibility for this piece of nature. Accordingly, a house is a garden pavilion, a private canopy erected for a limited period of time. It does not grow like an organic body whose volume increases. If a house within the garden is to grow with time, then it is supplemented by another space.

The pentagonal shape of the volume takes into account the best views of the local landscape. Generous openings frame the most beautiful sceneries of the garden and the surroundings. The conception of the house is thus based on the most expensive asset of the Viennese Hausberge – the view. The views in and out, captured by window frames, are key elements of the formal design. In addition, special emphasis was placed on the privacy of the residents. They can enjoy the views without being observed themselves.

1

2

1 The porch frames the entrance to the building.

2 The vestibule creates a transition between indoors and outdoors.

1

2

3

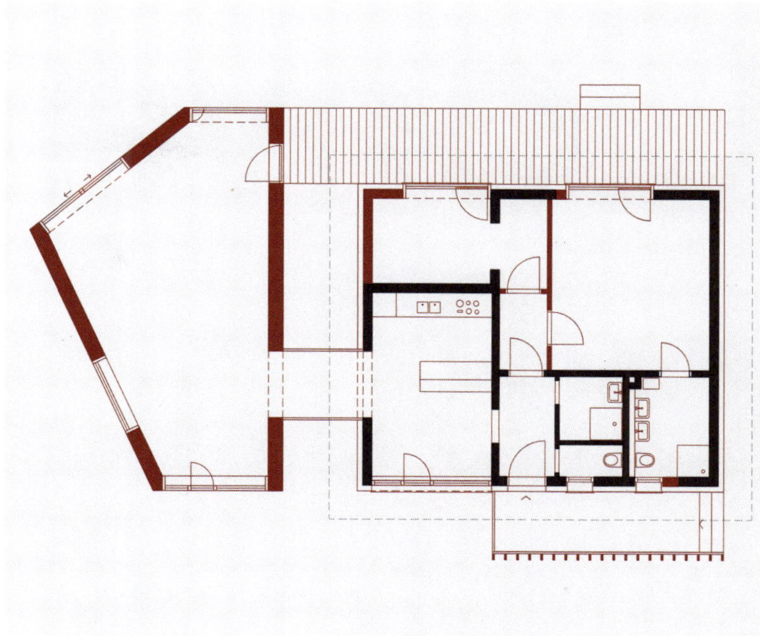

4

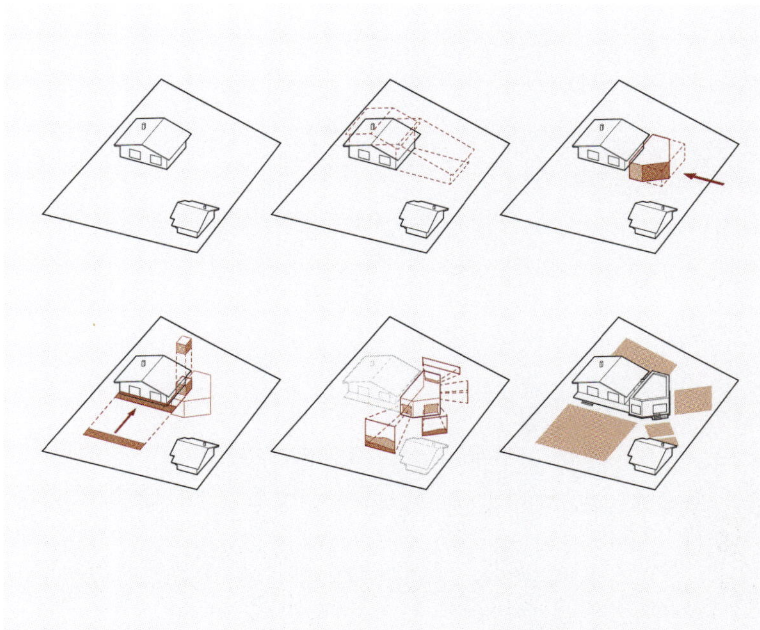

37

ARCHITECT
Jadric Architektur

COMPLETION
2020

ORIGINAL BUILDING
1969, Alfred Gölles

GROSS FLOOR AREA BEFORE | AFTER
65,18 m² | 126,35 m²

NUMBER OF ROOMS BEFORE | AFTER
3 | 4

1 The views inside and out, framed by the windows, are key elements of the formal design.

2 The glass paneled cube connects the existing building with the annex.

3 Ground floor plan

4 Diagram of the remodeling

Conversion of a Bungalow

Erkrath, Germany

The task was to renovate the core of a bungalow from the 1970s with a basement and to optimize it for a family of three.

38

The task of this project was to renovate the core of a bungalow from the 1970s with a basement and to optimize it for a family of three. Everything was demolished except for the basement and part of the load-bearing exterior walls of the shell – the rest was rebuilt or installed accordingly. The most relevant measure for the living spaces was the new construction or raising of the entire roof. Integrated skylights provide sufficient natural light even in rooms with exceptional depth, such as the dining area and the bathrooms.

Another new feature is the opening of the kitchen to the living and dining room and its lateral extension into the entrance area. As a result, the new staircase has a circular side wall surrounding it. The higher bedrooms for the child and parents were made more spacious, each with their own bath, with the parents additionally provided a dressing room. Apart from the renovation of the single apartment, the basement received a fitness area and a small office. Furthermore, the entire building front area with stairs and driveway as well as the garden and terrace area were also newly designed and built by Georg Döring Architekten.

1 The new entrance area is spacious and light-flooded.

1

1

2

3

38

ARCHITECT
Georg Döring Architekten

COMPLETION
2020

ORIGINAL BUILDING
1973

GROSS FLOOR AREA BEFORE | AFTER
390 m² | 390 m²

NUMBER OF ROOMS BEFORE | AFTER
5 | 6

4

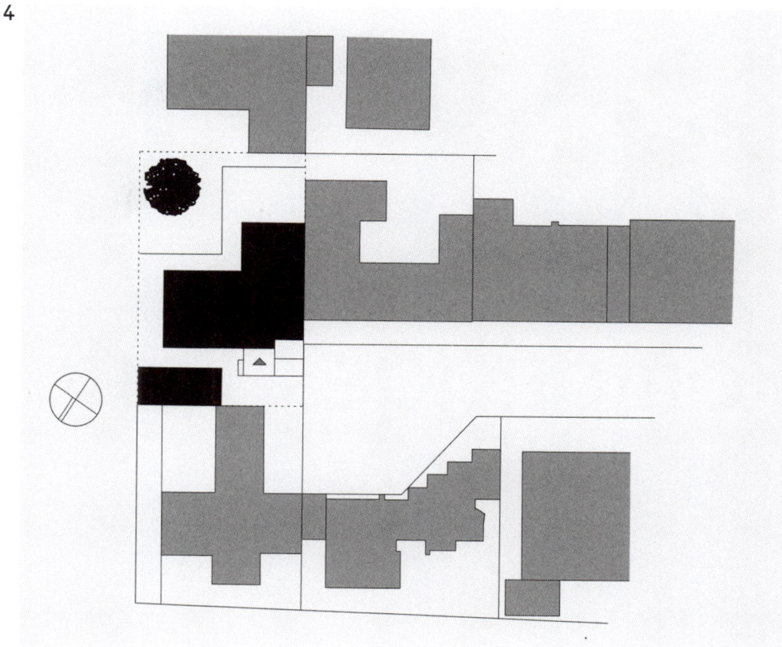

5

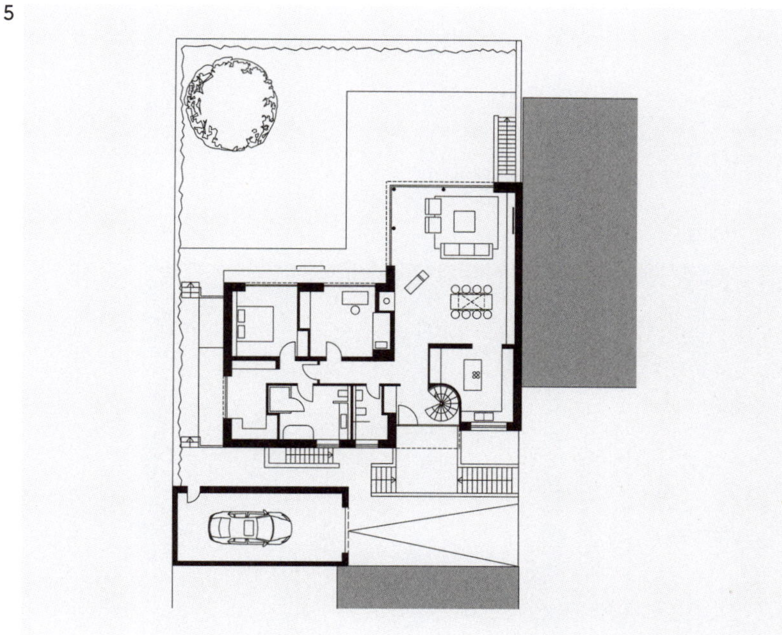

1 The new fireplace adds to the minimalistic furnishing.

2 The renewed staircase connects the floors.

3 Light globes are integrated into the ceiling of the living room.

4 Site plan

5 Ground floor plan

Box House

Romarigães, Portugal

Proposed was a contemporary volume, that explores the tension between existing and new.

39

A rehabilitation project always represents the conflict between the memory of past experiences and the urges of contemporary living. The existing volume has a singular configuration – rigid in shape and rudely built, similar to the typical Minho house. It's a building that intimately relates to the site where it is located, a kind of unsophisticated but charming rural "plaza". In this context, a new and contemporary volume, with the intention to cause contradicting feelings to the observer, was proposed. Its color, materialization, shape and position, causes a purposeful distinction between the old and the new.

The purpose of this project is a single family house, with the program developed in two levels: social spaces on the lower floor, two bedrooms and a bathroom on the upper floor. On the lower floor, kitchen, dining and living room are organized in sequence from north to south. Abundant space is organized both by a central enclosed storage volume – protecting the kitchen's work area – and by the stairs that access the upper floor. These stairs present themselves as an ornamental element, a sculptural piece in concrete and wood that separates the dining from the living space. The upper floor is divided into two bedrooms and a bathroom. One on the north elevation and the other on the south, both rooms are symmetrical, with the same dimensions, respecting the constant symmetry of the plan. All of these spaces – bedrooms, bathroom, and storage – are closed and independent. For this reason and with the intention of simplifying the interior, both walls and doors are covered in natural wood cladding to create more uniform surfaces. Without any expansion to the original footprint, the program is organized within the remaining boundaries, assuming the existing relationship between interior and exterior.

1

1 3ox House is organized within the
-emaining boundaries, without any
expansion to the original footprint.

1

2

3

39

ARCHITECT
Tiago Sousa

COMPLETION
2019

ORIGINAL BUILDING
1910

GROSS FLOOR AREA BEFORE | AFTER
79 m² | 79 m²

NUMBER OF ROOMS BEFORE | AFTER
1 | 2

4

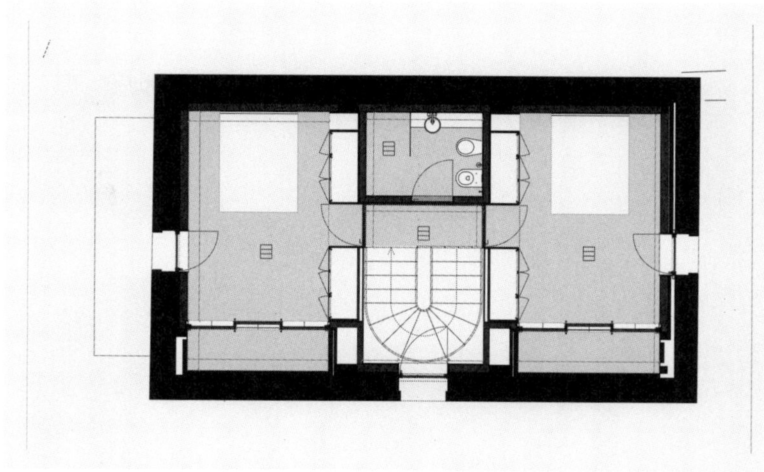

5

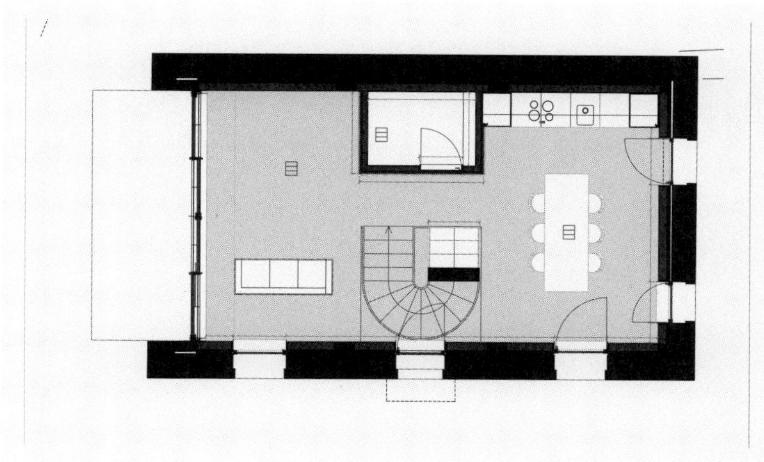

6

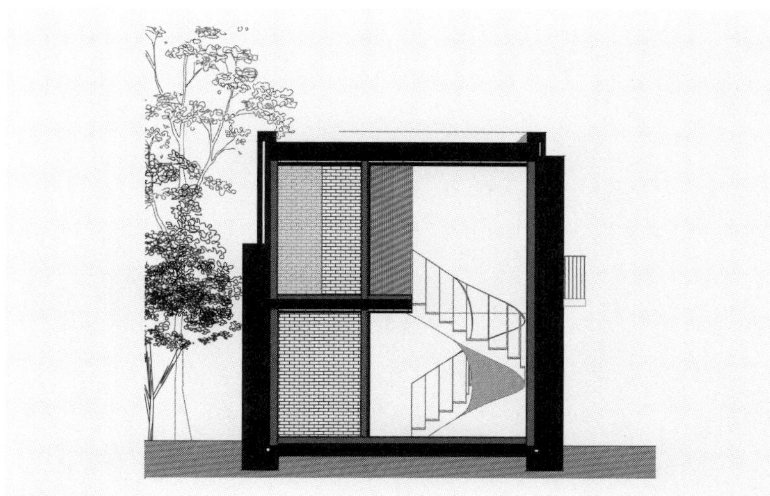

1 The contrast between old and new is the main focus of the project.

2 Natural stone walls emphasize the historic character of the building.

3 The staircase with its curvilinear design connects ground and upper floor.

4 First floor plan

5 Ground floor plan

6 Section

The Parchment Works

Northamptonshire, UK

The reconstructed house integrates the ancient ruins as a functional part of its design.

40

The existing property consisted of a Grade II listed double fronted Victorian house. Connected to the house was a disused cattle shed and beyond that a ruin, which was a former parchment factory listed in Northamptonshire as a monument to be preserved. The initial brief was to convert the cattle shed and demolish the ruin to make way for a new extension. The ruin was first viewed as a constraint as opposed to a positive asset that could be celebrated through a sensitive but well-conceived intervention. Instead of demolishing the ruin, Will Gamble Architects proposed a building within a building where two lightweight volumes could be delicately inserted within the masonry walls in order to preserve it.

A palette of simple materials was chosen both internally and externally which references the site's history and the surrounding rural context. Externally, weathering steel, oak, and reclaimed brick were used. The extension was built from upcycled materials predominantly found on-site, which was both cost effective and sustainable, whilst allowing the proposal to sensitively blend into its surroundings. Internally the structural beams of the existing cattle shed were exposed, as well as the steelwork to the new parts. The stone walls were repointed and washed in lime to create a mottled effect, and a concrete plinth was cast along the base to create a monolithic skirting. A contemporary kitchen, also designed by the practice, juxtaposes the uneven and disordered nature of the ruin and continues the theme of a modern intervention set within a historic context.

1 Modern and old go hand in hand while still clearly distinguishing themselves from each other.

1

1

2

3

4

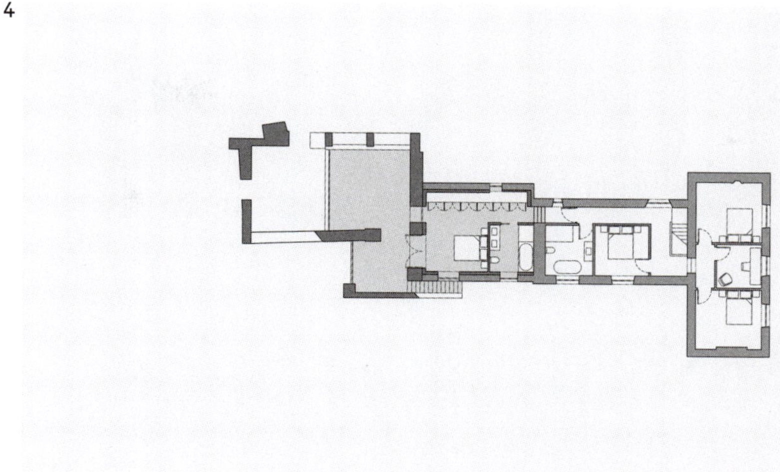

5

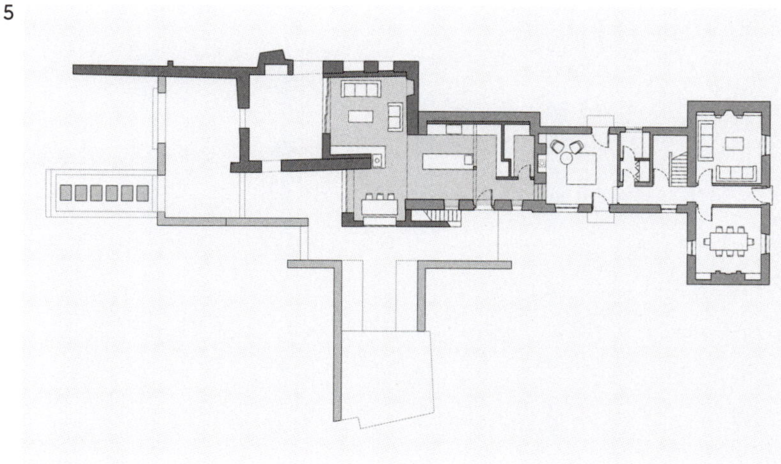

40

ARCHITECT
Will Gamble Architects

COMPLETION
2019

ORIGINAL BUILDING
16th century

GROSS FLOOR AREA BEFORE | AFTER
177 m² | 282 m²

NUMBER OF ROOMS BEFORE | AFTER
9 | 13

1 The joinery starkly contrasts to the original structure of the cattle shed.

2 The picture window marks the boundaries of the dining space.

3 The simplistic bespoke kitchen focuses the gaze on the original wooden ceiling.

4 First floor plan

5 Ground floor plan

Urban Beat

Montreuil, France

In contrast to tabula rasa, this project adds to the existing structure with a respectful and sustainable approach.

41

The generational family home is part of an inheritance and needed to be refurbished as well as preserved for future generations. The architects thus decided that an expansion would best allow the conservation of the existing structures while also adding space for the current residents.

The expansion consists of two differently sized blocks, each clad in poplar and pine – a simple but expressive composition. The new silhouette of the row of house resembles an urban heartbeat, integrating the new shape of the building harmoniously. Wood was chosen as the material of the new structure because of its light and environmentally friendly qualities along with its fast and easy assembly. Its texture is also an ideal visual addition to the existing dense context of the neighborhood.

The simplicity and sobriety of the façade unravel a rich yet subtle interior. The height variation of the new blocks created the opportunity to explore natural light sources in accordance with the space orientations and their immediate surroundings. An opening in the ceiling created by this height difference lights the bedroom while natural light from generous windows flood the double-volume staircase at the heart of the house.

1 This unique bookshelf optimally exploits the otherwise unused space under the staircase.

1

1

2

3

41

ARCHITECT
WY-TO architects

COMPLETION
2015

ORIGINAL BUILDING
1950

GROSS FLOOR AREA BEFORE | AFTER
40 m² | 80 m²

NUMBER OF ROOMS BEFORE | AFTER
4 | 6

4

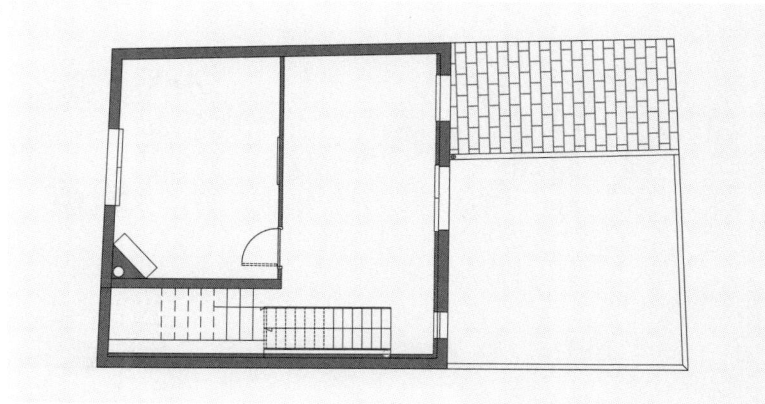

5

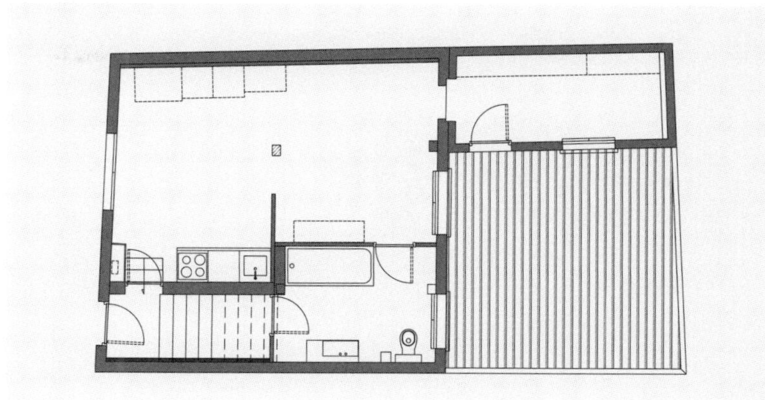

6

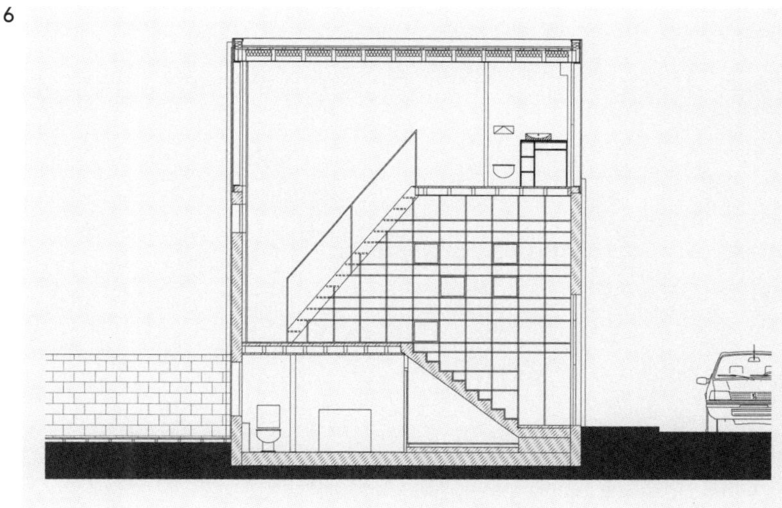

1 The façade maintains the intimacy of this home while letting in light.

2 The blinds are smartly integrated in the outer wall without disturbing the overall design.

3 Fine and poplar compliment each other while emphasizing the volumetric play.

4 First floor plan

5 Ground floor plan

6 Section

The House Recast

London, UK

The rear façade has been completely transformed by the innovative concrete structures, with the original brick wall being kept in tact where possible.

42

The brief was to reconsider the piecemeal rear façade of an end-of-terrace Victorian house in North London and to provide a new kitchen and two new bathrooms, one to be accessible on the ground floor. Studio Ben Allen was encouraged to use the project as a testbed for ideas. They wanted to push the boundaries of off-site fabrication – something that they felt was lacking in smaller scale residential or alteration projects.

The architects considered how to demonstrate exemplary use of pigmented patterned concrete as both structure and architectural finish on the extension. This approach was inspired by the surrounding Victorian architecture, in which the masonry is patterned and decorated, and at the same time is a load-bearing material that has the advantage of being fast and high quality, since it is manufactured off-site. The pattern on the main façade is mirrored in the balustrade, which was CNC cut by the architects and delivered as an easy-to-assemble kit of parts. Green patterned columns and beams create a framework for the salmon-colored structural wall panels of the first floor bathroom. Internally the use of pigmented concrete continues – with stairs, counters, sink, floors, benches, bath and washbasin all cast in pigmented concrete. Off-site fabrication shortened time on site, the main frame and walls of the extension being erected in just three days. A second theme of the project is the use of louvered, vaulted ceilings, which bring light down into both the kitchen and bathroom. A double height space connects the new ground floor spaces with a new mezzanine on the first floor, which in turn is connected to the main staircase. This void allows light to penetrate deep into the house while also creating visual and aural connections. Additional openings create similar connections from the living room, dining room and study to this central void on a smaller scale.

1 Everything from geometric, textural to color design is unique about this bathroom.

1

1

2

3

4

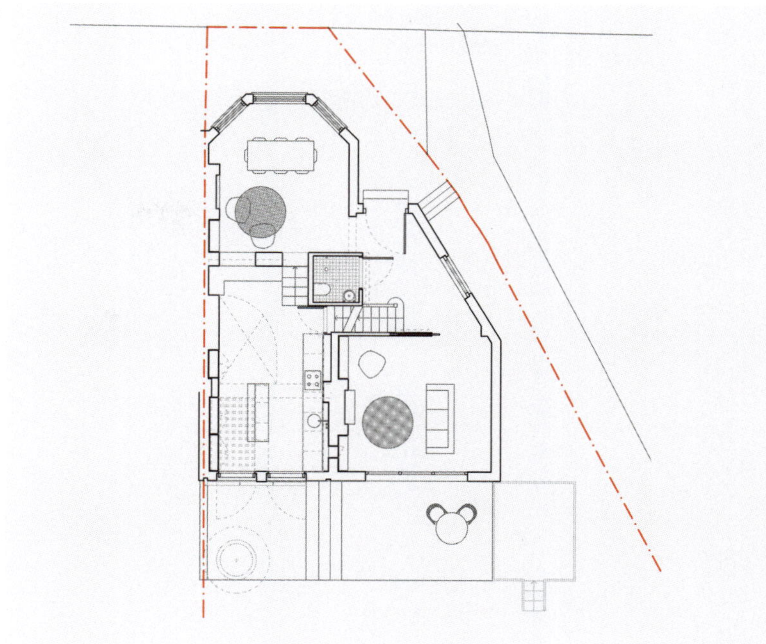

5

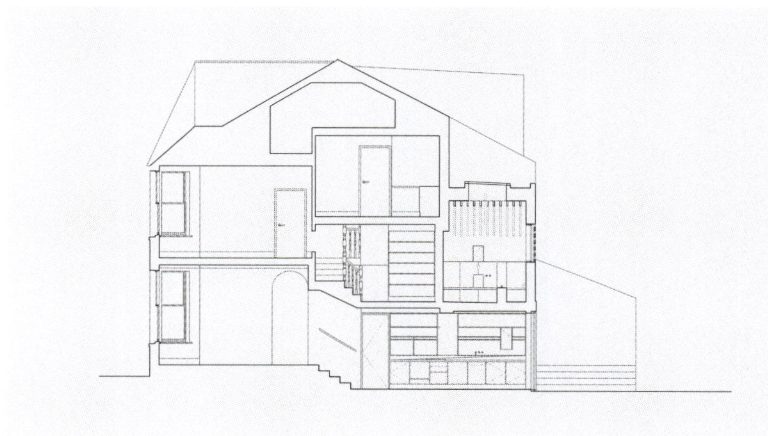

42

ARCHITECT
Studio Ben Allen

LANDSCAPE DESIGN
Daniel Bell

COMPLETION
2020

ORIGINAL BUILDING
1890s

GROSS FLOOR AREA BEFORE | AFTER
120 m² | 142 m²

NUMBER OF ROOMS BEFORE | AFTER
10 | 11

1 The void above the kitchen and its extension into the outside area create a dynamic spatial experience.

2 Strategically placed wall openings naturally guide light into the house.

3 The interior design lives from colorful cement accents.

4 Ground floor plan

5 Section

A

Bharat Aggarwal
p. 119–121

Javier Agustín Rojas
www.javieragustinrojas.com
p. 26, 27, 29, 30

Matthias Ammer
p. 161

Svend Andersen
p. 241, 243, 244

aNNo architecten
www.annoarchitecten.be
p. 44

Atelier Cais
www.ateliercais.pt
p. 112

atelier vanbelle
www.vensvanbelle.be
p. 94

B

Henning Baurmann
www.bdarchitekten.eu
p. 88

James Brittain
www.james-brittain.com
p. 125, 127, 128

C

Cameron Campbell Integrated Studio
www.integratedstudio.com
p. 207, 209, 210

Swen Carlin
www.swencarlin.com
p. 89–92

Yang Chaoying
p. 21, 23

David Jeremy Connor
www.davidconnordesign.co.uk
p. 170

Josema Cutillas
www.josemacutillas.com
p. 212–215

D

Johan Dehlin
www.johandehlin.com
p. 235, 237, 238

Luis Díaz Díaz
www.luisdiazdiaz.com
p. 101, 103, 104

Georg Döring
www.doering-architekten.de
p. 222

Filip Dujardin
www.filipdujardin.be
p. 131, 133, 134, 167–169

E

E2architekten
www.e2architekten.de
p. 66

Sabine Egler
p. 84

Assen Emilov
www.assenemilov.co.uk
p. 49–52

Shai Epstein
www.shaiepstein.co.il
p. 149, 151, 152

F

French + Tye
www.frenchandtye.com
p. 247, 249, 250

David Frutos
www.davidfrutos.com
p. 73, 75, 76

fuertespenedo arquitectos
www.fuertespenedo.com
p. 194

G

Vlaamse Gemeenschap
p. 166

Ralph Germann
www.ralphgermann.ch
p. 32

Adria Goula
www.adriagoula.com
p. 119, 121,122

Nahum Gutman
p. 148

H

Lionel Henriod
www.lionelhenriod.ch
p. 33, 35, 36

Hannes Henz
www.hanneshenz.ch
p. 61, 63, 64

Hindley and Co
www.hindleyandco.com.au
p. 188

Jack Hobhouse
www.jackhobhouse.com
p. 137, 139, 140

I

I/O architects
www.ioarchitects.com
p. 48

J

Mladen Jadric
www.jadricarchitektur.at
p. 216

Jonathan Tuckey Design
www.jonathantuckey.com
p. 124

Barbara Joseph
p. 45 below, 46 left, 47

K

Michael Kai
www.michaelkai.net
p. 155, 157, 158

Yasutaka Kojima
www.yasutakakojima.com
p. 217, 219, 220

Koyori
www.koyori-n2.com
p. 182

L

Martin Lejarraga
www.lejarraga.com
p. 72

Lv Bo
p. 24

M

Mitsuori Architects
www.mitsuori.com
p. 154

João Morgado
www.joaomorgado.com
p. 177, 179, 180

James Morris
www.jamesmorris.info
p. 171, 173, 174

MWA Hart Nibbrig
www.mwahartnibbrig.com
p. 85–87

N

National Institute of Anthropology and History of Mexico. Sn-32. Secretaria de Cultura -INAH- Fototeca Constantino Reyes-Valerio -MEX- Colección Cajas Rojas. Nov. 1978.
p. 176

Neumann Monson Architects
www.neumannmonson.com
p. 206

Francisco Nogueira
www.francisconogueira.com
p. 113–116

P

Gonçalo Duarte Pacheco
www.goncaloduartepacheco.pt
p. 142, 143, 145, 146

Iván Paul
p. 78

Luis Pereira Miguel
www.pm-arq.com
p. 14

Ema Peter
www.emapeter.com
p. 201, 203, 204

Pavel Planicka
www.31architekti.cz
p. 38, 39, 41, 42

Tatjana Plitt
www.tatjanaplitt.com
p. 189, 191, 192

PLP Atelier
www.plpa.es
p. 8

R

Rute Raposo
www.ruteraposo.pt
p. 15–18

Michael Reisch
www.michaelreisch.net
p. 67, 69, 70, 223, 225, 226

Thomas Rudolf
p. 163, 164

Irene Ruiz
p. 79, 81, 82 above right, 82 below

S

Héctor Santos-Díez
www.santos-diez.com
p. 9, 11, 12, 195, 197, 198

architekturstudio Schroth
www.martinschroth.de
p. 107–110

Sergio Sebastián
www.sergiosebastian.es
p. 82 above left

Peter Semmer
p. 106

Andrea Solé
www.andreasole.com
p. 118

Studio Ben Allen
www.studiobenallen.com
p. 246

T

André Tavares
www.andretavares.net
p. 54

Ivo Tavares Studio
www.ivotavares.net
p. 229, 231, 232

Arménio Teixeira
www.armenioteixiera.com
p. 55, 57, 58

TIANJIE GROUP
p. 20

U

Junichi Usui
www.instagram.com/jusui
p. 183, 185, 186

V

Hannelore Veelaert
www.hanneloreveelaert.com
p. 45 above, 46 right above

Tim Van de Velde
www.tvdv.be
p. 95, 97, 98

W

Wespi de Meuron Romeo Architekten BSA AG
www.wdmra.ch
p. 60

Will Gamble Architects
www.willgamblearchitects.com
p. 234

WY-TO
www.wy-to.com
p. 240

ISBN 978-3-03768-275-3

www.braun-publishing.ch

1st edition 2022

Editor: Chris van Uffelen
Editorial staff and layout:
Thúy-Nhiên Juliane Pham, Maja Ellen von Hasseln
Graphic concept: KOSMOS – Visuelle Kommunikation / Martin Denker
Reproduction: Bild1 Druck GmbH, Berlin

Cover front (from left to right, from above to below): Fraher & Findlay Architects, Jack Hobbhouse; Hindley and Co; Tatjana Plitt
Cover back: (from left to right) I/O architects; Assen Emilov